Pare[nti]ng *TEENS* in a Confusing Culture

Answering Parent's Most Challenging Questions

Parenting *TEENS* in a Confusing Culture

Answering Parent's Most Challenging Questions

Mark Gregston
Foreword by Tim Kimmel

Heartlight Ministries
FOUNDATION
P. O. Box 480 Hallsville, Texas 75650
www.HeartlightResources.com

Parenting Teens in a Confusing Culture
Copyright © 2008 by Mark Gregston
Published by Heartlight Ministries Foundation
P.O. Box 480
Hallsville, Texas 75650
www.HeartlightResources.com

Library of Congress Cataloging-in-Publication Data
Gregston, Mark, 1955 –
        Parenting Teens in a Confusing Culture
Cover design by Bethany Press
This book contains stories in which the author has changed some names and
identifying details in order to protect the privacy of those mentioned.
All Scripture quotations, unless otherwise indicated, are taken from the Holy
Bible, New International Version®. NIV®. Copyright © 1973, 1978, 1984 by
International Bible Society. Used by permission of Zondervan. All rights reserved.
Printed in the United States of America.

Dedication

Dedicated to my daughter, Melissa
And her husband, Blake, their two daughters,
Maile and Macie,
And my son, Adam.
You bless me in ways you'll never know!

Acknowledgements

A special thanks to the following people who participate in all the workings of a ministry dedicated to providing resources to families in need of which this book is a small part:

To Jan, my wife; you keep me laughing and loving life.

To all the Heartlight Staff for your commitment to kids and families. Your willingness to serve those who are struggling does not go unnoticed by those who benefit from your service, and from the One you serve. A special thanks to Blake Nelson, Ben Weinert, Emily Roberts, and our residential staff. A "Thank-You" to Pam Mitchell, Mary Hopkins, and Alison Hill who keep all the Heartlight staff on their toes, and offer each a wonderful friendship and spirit of encouragement to all of us. And a very special thanks to Tony and Ashley Michael, Kevin Shelby, and Susan Lewis, and David Fetherlin, who share their insight and wisdom with kids and parents daily.

To Melissa Nelson and Courtney Goswick who offer a helping hand to those who reach out in need. You both rock and are a true reflection of the One who is our Rock.

To Sam Sheeley for your friendship, and your commitment to excellence in ministry to struggling teens and their families, and your heart of gold.

To Tammee Bolthouse for your wonderful insights, heartfelt observations, and for your willingness to share those through newsletters and articles. You're touching the hearts of thousands!

To Dave Bolthouse for your magical touch and brilliant crafting of our message to the masses. Your accomplishments are changing the lives of families everywhere.

To the Heartlight Ministries Foundation Board of Directors, George and Livia Dunklin, Jerry and Leanne Heuer, Bill and Jeanie O'Connell, and Bill and Susanne Walsh, for your commitment to helping parents in need find the help and hope they search for.

To the Heartlight Ministries Board of Directors, Joe and Jana Crawford, Mike and Carol Barry, David and Amy Muth, Mike and Dianne Puls, and Raymond and Cindy Russell who help make the Heartlight Residential program one of the best in the country.

To Roger Kemp and Company, Wayne Shepherd, and Joe Carlson who help get the word "out" through radio. "We be mass communicatin!" It's an honor to be able to work with you.

To Natalie Gillespie for your help in correcting my bad grammar and getting my thoughts in order.

Contents

What Parents Can Do to Mentor and Guide Their Teen

Foreword

A couple of years ago, I spent a couple of days drift boat fishing on the Snake River. Each day I was assigned a different guide to row the boat and coach me along. My first guide was a man who had an extraordinary talent for catching fish. Unfortunately, he lacked skill in transferring any of his extraordinary talent to me. He got impatient when I didn't grasp what he was trying to teach me right away. We were contending with a lot of wind, yet he got irritated when I'd under-cast or forget one of the many steps in the process. About halfway through this first day, it was obvious that I was being coached by a man who lacked much respect for me as a novice and had little confidence in my ability to get the hang of it. My incompetence annoyed him. At the end of the day, we only had a couple of fish for our efforts. He blamed our poor showing on the fact that I simply "didn't get it."

Then there was the next day. Same river, same boat, and same weather conditions. But this time, I had a guide who obviously loved what he did. He also had great confidence in my potential to rise to the challenge. He spoke hope, taught through the power of encouragement, and showed a great respect for me as both a student and a person.

It was a day of nonstop catch-and-release.

Walking through the valley of the shadow of adolescence with your kids is a whole lot more difficult than fly fishing will ever be. The problems our teenagers contend with can break our hearts as well as frighten us out of our wits. We need *help*, not lectures; *hope*, not just nice theories.

You hold in your hand a book filled with both of these wonderful assets. And it's written by a man who has a great respect for you as a parent. Mark Gregston's never met a teenager he can't believe in or a parent he doesn't want to help become better. He knows that we all walk on feet of clay and sometimes contribute to the conditions surrounding our teenager's problems. Yet he consistently responds to our pleas for help with a high degree of respect and honor for us.

Mark has a clear "big picture" grasp of effective parenting. It's formatted by the power of God's grace and seasoned from decades of experience. His answers are candor bathed with compassion. Regardless of where your teenager is at this time, there's respect, encouragement, and hope waiting for you in *Parenting Teens in a Confusing Culture.*

Dr. Tim Kimmel
President, Family Matters

Introduction: Answering the Challenging Questions

The questions in this book are all-too-familiar to us at Heartlight, and I have answered them out of my experiences of interacting with and getting to know thousands of teens over the years. My intent is not to be a know-it-all. I'm not and never have been. (Ask just about anyone who knows me, and they'll confirm that.) But I have been told that I'm "a lot smarter than I look," so I'm going to take a stab at answering some of the questions that have come my way. I'm a guy who has worked with hundreds of families struggling through really tough issues, and I've had the good fortune to be able to live long enough to see the result of good counsel (and the bad fortune to see what happens as the result of bad counsel). I've seen what works in some situations and what doesn't work in others, and I've lived amidst a group of up to fifty kids at a time who have come and gone over the last twenty years to the residential ranch of Heartlight Ministries. By living with these teens, I have been able to pick up some insights and pointers because I have been surrounded constantly by the challenges and issues facing today's teens and their families.

I've always said that I would never write a book until I had a little gray hair and was over fifty. I have accomplished and am proud of both those benchmarks. And I've learned along the way that there are really no "pat" answers to questions that people ask. I believe that there are mind-sets, strategies, and approaches that work in some instances. I believe there are standards that should not be violated, principles that should not be given up, and Biblical mandates that should not be forgotten. I believe there are some strategies that are wrong. I believe that there are some traditions that are foolish, and there are some styles of parenting that just aren't going to work with today's teens.

I am not one of those guys who will find everything wrong with what you are doing as a parent and then leave you hangin' with no practical advice on what to do differently. I *am* a guy who believes that pain isn't always a bad thing, that kids are overly entitled and demanding, and that many parents are enabling their children to continue their foolish thinking. I believe that our generation of parents has spoiled our kids rotten, given them too much, and not expected enough. I believe that our generation has created a generation of immature kids who would rather act childishly than grow up, be given things rather than work for them, and have all the privileges of adulthood without accepting the responsibilities that go with it.

But don't be too hard on yourself. What most Christian parents today have done extremely well are the two most important things of all: They have built relationships with their kids that they did not have with their parents, and they've done a wonderful job of building values, developing character, and teaching their kids scriptural truth.

Still, many kids aren't making it spiritually, emotionally, academically and in many other ways through their teen years. Parents have done great things, but now they find themselves asking questions. And they are tough questions—questions about what to do when faced with pornography or substance addiction, same-sex attraction or overall laziness.

I have divided these main questions that I am asked time and again at seminars, on the radio, and at Heartlight, into three main categories. And I will address thirty-two specific questions to hopefully share some insights gathered throughout the turning-gray years that I have spent pouring into the lives of teens. I pray that I can shed some light on your situation and help you with your relationship with your child. I want you to see that the seeds you have sown in your child's life will come to fruition.

Would you believe me if I told you that the struggle you are now facing may be the greatest thing in your life? I doubt it. I didn't believe it when someone told me that same thing when I was going through a tough time. But just as sure as I am of the Scripture that reminds us that God has a plan for our lives (Jeremiah 29:11), that's how sure I am that you'll get over this "bump in the road" that your family is experiencing.

One day, I am convinced you'll thank God not only for getting you through it, but also for allowing you to endure it because it produced a new depth to your relationship with your child—and with God. The adolescent years provide plenty of opportunities for growth of parents and their kids.

The situations kids can get into during adolescence create lots of questions that force parents to seek answers. Because I have lived with, mentored, observed and listened to thousands of teens, I'll do my best within these pages to answer some of your toughest questions.

WHEN GOOD KIDS
GO WRONG

QUESTION 1

Help! Can You Save My Teen?

You're fired!" Those are two words that people never want directed at themselves, but love to watch being said to others on the popular TV series, *The Apprentice*. I'm no exception. I don't know why I like watching a show that rejects people for being inferior and always makes contestants feel a sense of rejection. But I do know this. There's something about those two words that conveys a special message to the ears of the one hearing them:

You're no longer worthy. You're a failure. We don't want you. You didn't do it well enough. You didn't make the mark. You are a loser. You are wrong. You can't do anything right. We're better off without you.

The impact is even worse.

If you're the one who got fired, questions begin to flood your thoughts. Your dreams are gone.

It's not working out the way that I thought it would. Could I have wasted my time? How could I have been so stupid? What's wrong with me? I must not be any good. I must be a failure.

You feel lost, alone, helpless, without hope, and you temporarily wonder what to do next, who to trust now, and who to talk to. Someone just pulled the rug from underneath you, and you feel betrayed, violated, and confused.

These are the same emotions that parents who are struggling with their teen feel every day. They are the same comments that hurting parents with hurtful and hurting teens say to me every day. The feelings of being fired are much like the feelings of parents coming to the realization that what they thought parenting was going to be, and what it has actually become, are two distant realities. And when they realize that their parenting skills aren't working or the outcome isn't what they expected, that message of being "fired," and the sense of loss and inferiority that accompanies it, become very real.

I understand.

That's how I felt when I heard those two words— "You're fired"—twenty years ago.

I was working for a ministry that I loved and poured my heart into. I was living in the small city of Branson, Missouri, where I fell in love with the people, the ministry, and the setting where I worked. I thought that I was doing well. I thought that my efforts were producing something worthwhile. And I thought that my relationships were fine. Just fine. Then out of the blue came those two words that changed my life.

The first people who came to my door to wrap their arms around me as I fell apart were Joe and Debbie Jo White. My wife Jan and I had the great honor of living at the Whites' ministry, Kanakuk Kamp, for seven years while I was an Area Director for Young Life and on staff with another ministry in the area. When they visited, neither one said much. They listened and hurt with me and my wife as we mumbled through random thoughts like, "*What are we going to do now?*" and the like.

I don't remember much of the discussion, but I do remember when Joe looked directly at me from under his bushy eyebrows and, staring deep into my eyes, said, "Mark, this is going to be the greatest thing that's ever happened to you." I thought, at the time, that he was flat-out crazy. Obviously, he didn't understand what we had just been told. I felt like he was trying to paint a silver lining on a dark, dark rain cloud that had just stormed on us and extinguished any semblance of light in our hearts. His words echoed in my head for years as I fought the hurt and disappointment that surrounded what I thought was to be. I really felt like God had just abandoned us, and Joe was telling me that this was a great time for us! At the time, I understood neither God nor his servant, Joe.

I did begin to understand Isaiah 55:8, which states that God's ways are not our ways. I felt like I was learning that the hard way.

Then we moved to Texas to start Heartlight. And even though we knew that we were to work with kids and their families, both Jan and I still longed to be in Branson, where our dreams, we thought, were to have been fulfilled. Jan fought living in the woods, and I fought depression, not sure that this new thing called Heartlight was "it" and not totally convinced that God knew what He was doing.

It wasn't until years later when Joe's father, Spike White, dropped in to see us as he was traveling through Texas in search of the next adventurous river to kayak, that the light of understanding began to dawn. As we walked the Heartlight property, he looked at me from under bushy eyebrows (even bushier than Joe's, so you know where Joe got 'em) and said, "Have you thanked him yet?" I thought he was talking about God, so I asked him if that was what he meant. He said he was talking about the man that fired me! I told him that I hadn't. He told me that I would one day. I thought, *Yeah, right.*

Okay, here's the point: Years after being fired and feeling like a failure, I can now look at my life, my work, and my happiness in fulfilling God's purpose for my life and see how right the Whites were. If I had never been fired, I probably would not be writing books, speaking around the country, sharing on a weekly radio program that airs on over 500 stations, and giving little daily snippets of information about parenting teens on more than 3,000 stations. I never thought that I would be leading seminars, speaking at events, or having the honor of serving the 2,000 families we've served at Heartlight.

And it all started from a point in time when I felt hopeless, lost, and unsure of where to turn. It was at that point that I not only started asking big questions about my life, but also started listening to the answers that were being given to me.

If you're struggling with your teen, you know how it feels to be "fired." It's a disheartening time of parenting when you may feel like all your hard work was useless, and you've lost one of your most precious possessions.

Can I save your teen?

The short answer is "no"—No one can save your teen but the Lord. But I can give you some insight, tools and some "expert" advice—often from the mouths of former troubled teens themselves—that will help you hang on for the roller coaster ride of the teen years and will hopefully improve your relationship (and your parenting) going forward.

You may not know it, feel it, understand it, or welcome it right now, but I can assure you that the struggle you are going through with your teen just might be the best thing that has ever happened in your life. Hard to believe, isn't it? Here's another thing that might be hard to believe: One day you will thank your child for the struggle, because you will be in a better place, and your relationship with your child will be deeper, stronger, and maybe, just maybe, more in line with what God desires for your relationship with your teen.

QUESTION 2

What Do I Do If My Teen Is Drinking?

"If we know our 15-year-old daughter is drinking, and she's doing it with her best friends, what do we do?"

Most young people I know don't do things *because* of their friends. They do things *with* their friends. Rarely do I see one young person overtly influence or put pressure on a peer. What I see more of is a teen's desire to belong, to connect, and to have friends. Pursuing these goals, a teen might pick up the habits of those they desire to connect with, but it is the teen's desire to be part of a group that should be the main focus, not the fact that they may be participating in the similar and unacceptable behavior of their peers.

Let me give you a simple example:

A group of teens smokes cigarettes. Your teen wants to connect with that group of teens. The fact that your teen chose that smoking group to connect with is a much larger issue than this particular smoking group influencing your teen. Instead of thinking that your child is picking up bad habits from a group of friends, a healthier perspective might be to consider whether your teen just might be encouraging his or her new friends to continue in their behavior. Remember, each teen in the smoking group has parents—and they are just as likely to be thinking that it's your kid who is the bad influence as you are to think it is theirs.

My point is that taking away friends doesn't eliminate the issue at hand. Eliminating friends doesn't solve the problem. The knee-jerk reaction of most parents is to get their child away from anyone who is a negative influence by saying, "You can't hang out with those kids anymore." But taking away friends doesn't mean the problem is going to go away. Your teen will just find another group with which to do the same thing, and you, as the parent, will run out of "acceptable" friends long before you find the "right" group for your teen to hang with.

I know all the sayings: "Bad company corrupts good morals," "If you swim with sharks, you're going to get bit," "Better to be alone than in bad company," and "Show me your friends, and I will show you who you are." There are plenty of them out there. And I agree with the Bible when it says that bad company can corrupt good morals. But I do not agree when a parent thinks it is all the fault of others, that their teen would be perfectly fine if it weren't for the others who are corrupting their child. Way too many times, unacceptable behavior is excused because of the influence of others.

You must deal with the issue at hand and not put the problem off on another teen or group of teens. That mentality takes away the responsibility that your child has for her participation in wrong behavior. And you might just miss the real issue at hand, therefore postponing the finding of a solution until the effects of the problem are greater. By then, you may have less influence and control of your child and the situation.

The Real Problem

Too often, parents think the way to get their kids to quit drinking it to simply tell them, "If you do this, then this will happen." That formula leaves out the opportunity for parents to uncover their teen's motivation for drinking, thus precluding some much-needed help. Teens drink alcohol for different reasons. What your child's reasons are should determine the consequences for the inappropriate behavior.

I'm not saying that teenage drinking is okay. You'll never find me writing or saying that. What I am saying is that it is crucial to find out *why* your teen has made the choice to drink so that you can accurately and effectively determine the appropriate consequences. Is your daughter drowning out emotional pain, trying to fit in with a crowd, or has she discovered that she loves the feeling of being drunk? Each of those motivations is very different and should be addressed differently.

Your consequences for drinking alcohol might need to include more than the typical grounding or taking away privileges, and be expanded to include random alcohol testing, counseling, earlier curfews, breathalyzer starters on a car, medications, additional positive social activities, or alcohol treatment.

If your teen's drinking is determined by you to be just an experimental thing, then let it be just that. Sit down and talk with your family members about how you feel about drinking and how you're going to handle it. I've seen many times where parents overreact to a relatively small issue, and a teen then counteracts. When that happens, parents find themselves dealing with a much larger problem. I've even seen some parents overreact and mete out the punishment equivalent of firing a cannon, when all that was really needed was a flyswatter. It's called making a mountain out of a molehill. Don't make it more than it is, but never allow it to be less than it is.

The key to finding that balance is this: *A gentle approach always turns away an overreaction.*

Now let me address the pink elephant that is sitting here in the room. Chances are, your teen will drink sometime during the high school years. Some parents know it. Some parents will never admit it. But just because they don't admit it, doesn't mean it doesn't happen. I am sure that, just as my parents didn't know everything that I did in high school, I don't know everything that my kids did during their high school years. Teens are curious. They experiment. They follow one another. They make bad choices. They make immature and impetuous choices. So don't be naïve parents.

I hear the wildest tales from normal Christian kids who are no different from those living in your home. If your child has made it through high school without partaking in the use of alcohol, consider yourself blessed that you haven't had to deal with that issue. (Of course, you might have to deal with it later when they leave home.)

If your child is drinking because they want to belong in a particular social arena, then you're seeing the desperation of your teen to "fit in." For them to drink and violate their values, your standards, and their own commitment not to drink shows the intensity of the desire to be part of the crowd. In this case, a discussion about the desire to fit in and what that can cost might remedy your teen's need to drink.

If your teen is drinking to feel normal because they're depressed most of the time, that's a very different story. The consequences for this type of behavior might include a trip to see a counselor or physician to help with depression. Many, many young people self-medicate. They drink illegally, when a doctor might be able to help them overcome the feelings of depression legally through prescribed medication, thus eliminating the need for drinking as a self-remedy.

Maybe your teen drinks alcohol to erase images that play in their minds. My wife was sexually abused for years. Her parents didn't know it until she was almost a teen. Has something happened that your teen may have chosen alcohol to help them forget? You'll never know if you don't ask.

I know many teens who drink to help them sleep at night. I know others who drink because they say it is the only time they aren't afraid. (This reasoning gives understanding to alcohol's nickname, "liquid courage.") Some teens drink because they feel like failures. Some drink because they are frustrated. Others drink because they want to escape. Teens manage their anger through drinking and drink because they want to become someone they're not. Many just like the feeling of getting a "buzz," getting drunk, being plastered. (I always like to ask teens who enjoy getting drunk why that particular feeling means so much to them.)

Until you know the reason why your teen is drinking, you might continue on a path of correction that will never remedy the current crisis.

So how do you find out what motivates your teen to drink?

Sit down and ask.

And if you don't have the kind of relationship that allows for that to happen, then you might have just found the answer. There is motivation behind every teen's actions. Understanding the motivation insures that your approach is correct and your consequences for this type of inappropriate behavior are practical, effective, and appropriate.

The Confusing Messages Surrounding Teen Alcohol Use

Teens live in a confusing world when it comes to drinking. They see beer commercials that make them laugh and want to drink a beer just for the fellowship the commercial displays. They see sports heroes and rock stars endorse beer. They see advertisements that display alcohol as attractive. Between hundreds of TV shows, millions of impressions on the Internet, and movies and videos that glamorize alcohol consumption, it's hard to believe that they are not influenced in some way.

Now let me go from preachin' to meddlin':

They see some parents who purchase their teens alcohol. They see churches that now serve wine at some of their church functions. They see Mom and Dad drink wine during meals. They read that Jesus turned water into wine. There's very little doubt in my mind that there is less of a taboo in the Christian world regarding alcohol consumption today than there was in years past. I'm not passing judgment on what you do or don't do, but I am telling you that it's a mixed message being sent to teens today. It's a confusing message. What used to be so black-and-white to us is all gray to them.

Because it's a gray area, I would encourage you to lean on a couple of principles that I have found to be helpful in discussing the issue of drinking.

First, I would let the teen know that you understand the difficult spot they are in, and I would have a conversation that goes something like this:

> I know that it's hard to say "no" to the things that you are faced with today. Believe me, I would not want to be growing up in your shoes. But I want you to know something that I hold dear, and that's the fact that I am against you consuming alcohol in any form. I do not believe it is right, and it is not legal. So I can't allow you to do this. One day you'll be able to make up your own mind about alcohol and make your own choices, but as long as you live here, I just can't let it happen.

Second, I would encourage you not to destroy your relationship with your child today because of actions on your teen's part that will, in a very short time, be legal (and in society's mind, "okay") for them. In the same breath, I would strongly encourage you not to allow your child to destroy himself with behavior that may get beyond his control.

You must be age-conscious *and* determine your child's motivation. Here are some examples: If you have a 12-year-old who is drinking, you probably have a much more serious problem than if you have a 17-year-old who is occasionally drinking. If you have a 16-year-old who comes home drunk every day from school, you have a much greater problem on your hands than a 15-year-old who just experimented with alcohol once or twice.

So what can a parent expect when it comes to drinking?

1. Don't be surprised if your teen comes home one night smelling of alcohol. Ready yourself for that time. It is probably best to sit down and talk with your teen the day after she comes home from drinking the night before.

2. Be understanding, but be firm. Perhaps you can share some experiences that you've had in your life in order to explain why you are so adamant about your rules and expectations. But don't let the foolish actions of your past be an excuse for your child to justify his actions (or for you to justify them)!

3. Ask questions to seek the motivation for the drinking.

4. Set firm consequences for drinking, and because you must follow through on your consequences when rules are broken, make sure that the consequences you set are enforceable. Make sure that you're willing to do what you say. If you say that you'll take away the car if you catch teens drinking, take away the car. If you say they're grounded for a month, ground them for a month. If you say that one of the consequences for continuing to make poor choices is that they'll have to start meeting with a counselor, then send them to a counselor. And if you ever say, "If you continue this behavior, then you won't be able to live at home," have a plan in place should they violate your standard.

5. Keep talking with your teen. Make every effort to keep the lines of communication open.

6. Instead of eliminating friends, embrace them. God might want to use you in the lives of your teen's friends. Tell

your daughter that she can hang out with her friends as long as they come over to your home and you get to know them. Add that she won't be hanging with them until that happens.

7. Talk to their parents. Inform them of what is happening. They're concerned for their teens as well. Treat them as you would want to be treated. Let them know your concerns and how you're willing to get through this time. What a wonderful time to get parents together to talk about their teens! Don't be afraid. You've been training all your life for this moment. To "tuck tail and run" is to avoid the very battle that God may be calling you to fight—and win. It's okay to fight for your child and to fight for good choices for your child's friends.

How you respond to your child during a first-time crisis like alcohol experimentation will reflect your commitment to them, and your commitment to God. Many times, people ask me how they can be used by God in this world. I tell them to live in the circles God has given them, not to be afraid to confront that which is wrong, to befriend those who are headed down a destructive path, and to be a light to those who are inching towards the darkness.

QUESTION 3

What If My Daughter Has a Girlfriend?

"We were shocked to read some of our daughter's e-mails and find that she is calling herself a lesbian and has a girlfriend. Initially, I thought that I was just reading some sort of joke, but after asking more questions and doing a little more snooping around, we have found this to be true. We're devastated! And the girl she's "in love" with is a girl that we've known for years. We're good friends with her parents. Is this just a dream, or is it the beginning of a nightmare? What are we supposed to do? We feel so helpless and lost. I don't think we could hear any worse news."

Let me assure you that you can hear worse news. As I was sitting down to write this chapter, I received news that the son of a friend of mine had just backed over his little sister with a car, and she died. The terrible loss of a 5-year-old daughter because of a simple mistake of a teenage son...I can't think of much that could be any worse than that. So, yes, one can hear worse news.

It is against this backdrop of loss that I would encourage you to approach your daughter. I know many families that would love to have the opportunity to struggle through issues with their daughters...teens who didn't live beyond their adolescent years. Whatever your daughter is going through, the fact that she is alive, coupled with the hope promised in God's Word, puts your situation in a position where timing becomes the bigger issue at hand as you walk this path. As troublesome as it may feel, you've got to keep it in perspective.

Just because she's making some bad decisions, being deceitful, and making some poor choices, doesn't mean she is any less precious in the sight of God, nor is she any less worthy of someone throwing her a lifeline in her time of need. Just because her problem happens to be one that is offensive to you or unacceptable to your values, your principles, and your desires for your daughter, doesn't mean she is any less worthy of your love. You may not support her in her decisions or ultimately her choice of lifestyle, but I would pray that you would never lose your love for her, nor a willingness to continue to pursue her in the midst of her struggle.

Here's the reason why:

Teens today are being influenced in so many different ways that many are confused, conflicted, and trying to make sense of a culture that is just as confused and conflicted. The sexually permissive nature of our society, coupled with the greater tolerance of homosexuality and the mind-set that is widely accepted that teens should do whatever they want, culminates in massive sexual confusion for adolescents.

It's not that the permissiveness of the culture *encourages* these same-sex relationships, but for the most part, the culture now no longer *discourages* this type of relationship. The longing to connect, the sexualization of the culture, the acceptance of alternative lifestyles, and the lack of discouragement from society all blend together to create a perfect storm.

In the midst of the storm, poor choices are made. One of those areas happens to be same-sex relationships—the idea of which is not nearly as foreign to teens as it is to parents.

If the parents in the example above allow their daughter's offensive actions to push her away, then the opportunity to bring a "lost sheep" back into the fold has been lost. If parents refuse to be part of the struggle their daughter is going through, who will speak truth into her life when she needs it the most? Who's going to be there for her when her life begins to fall apart and she's excluded and eliminated all her other friends? The answer, hopefully, is you. But not if you've erected a barrier because of her choices.

Some parents have the tendency to walk away from a teen who is involved in a same-sex relationship because the situation feels so foreign, and most refuse to believe that their daughter would willingly choose this path. Parents must become comfortable with being uncomfortable and not let the sin push them away from the sinner, who just happens to be, in this case, their precious child. Sure, she's made some wrong decisions that will take her to places she won't want to be. Remember, her "best thinkin'" has gotten her into the situation she's in, but chances are her "best thinkin'" is not going to be able to get her out.

Know What You Believe

Finding out your daughter is calling herself a lesbian (or that your son thinks he is gay) will force you to determine what you believe about same-sex relationships. I say same-sex purposefully, instead of lumping all of these relationships in the homosexual, gay, or lesbian category, because I believe that this current teen culture allows same-sex intimate interactions without calling yourself a homosexual. Just because you might see homosexual behavior doesn't mean that you're looking at a homosexual. But you will have to discover, if you haven't already, where you stand and what you believe about any type of same-sex orientation, lifestyle, or relationship. It's important to determine where you stand, because your stance will be tested as you deal with a teen in this situation.

So what do you believe? Is homosexuality a choice, or are people born into it? Is it a predisposition, but a person still makes the choice? Should same-sex marriages be allowed? Is heterosexual the only way to have a marriage?

When you face a child who is wrestling through same-sex issues, you need to know what you believe, because when discussions get heated, the opinions that you share will come back to haunt you. Your child's "coming out" forces you to come out as well.

If you believe that same-sex relationships are okay, then I'd just skip to the next chapter and forget about this one. If that's the case for you, let your teen do whatever he or she wants, and just wait and see what happens. This might be an easier path in the short run, but it's a more damaging one in the long run.

Now I'm not here to debate the homosexual issue. That question's been around for centuries; and I'm not going to be able to present all the medical, scientific, psychological, scriptural, and genetic data to justify it one way or the other. What you must determine for yourself is whether you believe that your child is living in a sinful manner by having a same-sex relationship. If you believe not, then walk away and let whatever happen, happen. But if you believe that what you are observing is sin, then to sit back and do nothing only allows your teen to sink deeper into a hole that will be too difficult to climb out of on her own.

I believe that God warns teens against sin, not because He's some policeman with an authoritative ego, but because He really doesn't want them to end up in a place they never wanted to be. He wants to help teens get to the place where they want to be and where He created them to be. It will help if this "sinner," as with any sinner, is surrounded by people who will be willing to fight for her.

Understanding Your Daughter's Attraction to Another Girl

Your teen might move toward same-sex relationships for a number of reasons. Please note that none of my suppositions are intended to justify same-sex relationships. My observations are shared with the hope that parents will gain a deeper understanding of why their child has chosen this path. I believe that a deeper understanding will help parents handle the situation positively, rather than pushing a child deeper into an unhealthy relationship. In other words, you don't want your child holding onto an unhealthy relationship just to prove to you that she can make decisions for herself and that you can't control her.

There are many reasons why a teen experiments with a same-sex relationship. There might be some confusion about sexual identity issues because of prior sexual abuse. Don't rule it out. Just as you didn't share with your parents everything that happened to you as you grew up, so your teen may have some secrets, too— some very painful ones. This possibility is essential to explore, as the root issue might not be the same-sex relationship, but some damage that has happened in the life of your child that is fueling her current choices.

If a girl has been raped and has a fear or hatred of men, that doesn't necessarily mean that she wants to remain isolated. We're all created with the desire to connect with people, and the intensity of that desire might play out in a damaged daughter's willingness to violate her own strongly held values and principles to have this need met.

Then there are those that choose to move into a same-sex relationship because that's what they like. The motivation for their "liking" may even be because they aren't given the opportunity to try anything different. I have recently seen numerous times where parents refused to let their daughter date or develop any type of relationship with a young man, and the result was that their daughter transferred her unfulfilled longings to her girlfriends.

Some girls just want to experiment with this new fad that they see and hear about. A few years ago, I watched three popular music stars named Britney, Christina and Madonna kiss on stage at the MTV Video Music Awards and was shocked at the ripple effect from their message that "this type of behavior is okay." Kids have now been imitating these three girls for years, and their irresponsible actions gave license and permission to every wannabe, impersonator, or easily influenced young girl that had a love of experimentation and an inquisitive nature.

Here's the problem that is created by their experimentation: It feels good. Their bodies respond in pleasure. When that happens, girls come to the conclusion that they must be gay—or that it must be right. Some girls then change their stance on what they thought and believed about same-sex relationships to accommodate their violation of their own principles. I mean, if you don't want to feel guilt or shame about your actions, just get rid of the principle or value that causes the conflict, and you'll never have to feel bad, right? This is what many teens do.

Parents recognize this change when they say, "How can she just give up what she's known to be right all her life?" or "She's always been against this; how can she change her beliefs so quickly?" or "This isn't the girl we know; things just changed overnight."

In their heart of hearts, teens know what is right and what is wrong. The seeds that have been sown by parents into the lives of their kids don't just all of a sudden die when teens state they don't believe anymore. Those seeds are still there, still alive, and still waiting to be nourished. They will grow...just as God has promised. This is why it is so important for parents, in their confrontation of their teen's same-sex relationship, to continue to provide a place of nurturing and growth while dealing with the inappropriate behavior and confused thinking.

There are also girls who just want to be different, and because a same-sex relationship is a way to be different, they choose to shock those around them with their new "Look-how-different-I-am-now" mentality and behavior. Teens want to be known for something. They want recognition. They want to stand out (and at the same time, to fit in. Go figure.) They want to make their own decisions.

I've always thought that this is one heck of a way to take a stance on all these desires, because most girls don't realize that the ripple effects of such choices will follow them throughout their high school years. What was intended by their actions to shock in their earlier high school years is not easily forgotten by guys in their later high school years. It's my observation that most high school guys avoid high school girls who have been involved in same-sex relationships. There are times that the high school social setting doesn't allow for change of perception to happen as quickly as some girls would like. So they are doomed to fulfill their role that they have constructed for themselves. They've made their bed; now they've got to lie in it.

This issue becomes particularly important when a girl is trying to break out of the mold that she has made for herself, and her current environment just won't let that happen. In this case, a parent may help a daughter with her transition by allowing her to move to a new setting—to stay with relatives, try a new school, go to a place like Heartlight, move in with friends in another town, or help her graduate early so that she can start a new life that is different from the one she created in high school.

Most of the time when Christian girls are involved in same-sex relationships, the relationship is a huge secret, and there is the additional thrill of the forbidden. The girls involved become consumed with each other because they've excluded everyone else. They defend each other to the death because they've got something "special" and they are the only ones who are "there for each other." They play off each other's emotions heavily. Their justification of their relationship never ceases to amaze me. The uniqueness of this relationship is far different from a young lady having a relationship with a young man. Even if that relationship is unhealthy or unapproved by parents, at least it's normal. And most Christian girls know that what they are doing in same-sex relationships has moved into the abnormal. To calm their own shame and guilt, they dive deeper into the relationship and move further away from those that they love, as if this movement is a coping mechanism that allows them to tolerate their own choices and actions.

Because of the secretiveness of the relationship and the consuming passion that girls will display for each other, it is of utmost importance that parents handle the confrontation of the relationship with a gentleness that doesn't force a child to "go dark." Going dark means that, in order to hide or cope with their own shame, teens leave their family and pursue their new life apart from everyone who has always loved and known them. They might become exclusive and private. They could disengage from family to ease the pain of having to face family members who pass judgment not in their words, necessarily, but by their mere presence. I'm not saying that this judgment is wrong. I'm just saying that your teen may feel and perceive judgment by the mere presence of other family members.

To reach your daughter, special care needs to be given that would invite a response, not demand it, that would encourage discussion, not force it. Be honorable and gentle in your approach, no matter how messed up your daughter's thinking happens to be at the moment.

Confronting the Issue

Before you jump to conclusions about what your daughter's relationship is with another girl, ask questions. Any suspicion you have needs to be investigated. Talk to her teachers. Ask your school officials to help. Read text messages. Read e-mails. Keep your ear to the ground and listen for what you would normally miss in conversation. Leave no rock unturned, and explore everything as you would seek out cancer. For this is a cancer, and it has the ability to change the course of the lives of each of your family members.

People always ask if they should pry and spy into the lives of their teen. My answer is an unequivocal "yes"! While you might trust your daughter to some degree, I hope you would also remember that she is an adolescent capable of making poor choices, being deceived by people, and being easily influenced in areas that could unravel all you have put together in your family.

Once you have some answers and are sure of your child's same-sex relationship, I would encourage you to let the truth of your findings sink in for a few days. Don't feel like you have to tackle everything the day you find out something. If you take the time to meditate on what you've discovered, pray about it, and seek wise counsel, you will have a better mind-set and understanding, lest you jump right in and say things you'll regret, or act upon feelings that will take years to resolve. Take your time, and trust that God will give you direction as you walk along the path of this conflict. He doesn't always give you an answer up front, but He promises not to leave you while you are walking through the process.

I would suggest that you have a series of meetings with your child and not try to talk about everything in one setting. These could be spread out over the course of one day, (depending on the severity of the situation), or they could be spread out over a period of a couple of weeks. Whichever you choose, be intentional and stick to your plan. Don't let a child's response deter your process of moving your daughter to an understanding of what your plan will be.

Before you meet the first time to confront her with what you have found or what she has shared with you, think through each of the meetings. Here is my suggestion for what should be covered in each: Use the first meeting to expose the issue and try to uncover your daughter's motivation, the second to express what you feel, and the third aimed at laying out your expectations. Covering everything at once will often confuse the way your daughter interprets your process. Remember, she isn't thinking clearly, so you'll have to be deliberate in your approach.

Exposure

The first meeting is to expose what you know, what you have found out, or what you have been told and have good reason to believe. It's a time to ask your daughter to sit down and talk. If both parents are present, then I'd encourage one person to take the lead. (Dads, don't lead a business meeting; and Moms, don't start blubbering and crying, or vice versa.) While the freedom to express emotions needs to be allowed to some degree, be intentional about the process of the meeting and what you are trying to accomplish.

The intent should be just to expose. The meeting should be lined out in such a way that you let your child know that you know, what you know, and what you don't know. And that's it. Statements like the following might give you some direction:

"Sarah, we have reason to believe that relationship that you have with 'x' has moved into an unhealthy one."

"Amy, the school called and said that they've seen you holding hands and kissing 'x' between classes."

"Lauren, there's something wrong that is happening, and it has to do with 'x'. We've looked at your text messages (or e-mails, or IM's) and see that your words to 'x' are scary to us."

"Rachel, the other night when we walked in on you and 'x' it was an affirmation of what we've thought we've been seeing."

"We know that your relationship with 'x' has moved from just friendship to something deeper, and we know that you've been physical with her. We don't know much beyond that, but we would love to be able to discuss this whole issue."

The mere fact that you know what is going on will hopefully get her thinking. It might be the wake-up call she needs that spurs her to repentance, or it might be the release of everything that Pandora's Box can throw at you. Expect her to be defensive, angry, ashamed, sad…Whatever the response, just let her think. If she starts asking you questions, tell her that you want to answer those but will address them after you've thought through your answers.

Tell her that you want to her to have time to think, too, and then you'll get back together to talk further. Tell her, *"I want you to think about what's going on, and we want to share with you what we feel and think. But let's do this in a couple of days."*

Once your daughter is confronted with the truth, she knows the "cat's out of the bag," and it can't be ignored. Your daughter may get mad that her scheme to keep you out of the loop is no longer working. She might feel betrayed if friends or teachers shared something with you. She might feel depressed now that she's exposed. Because she is ashamed, she might run. She might act out in anger. She might just deny it all—or hide in her room in shame. There is no way to predict what your child's response might be, so be prepared for anything.

Whatever the response, whether she is yelling at you or sulking in her room, keep reassuring her that you love her, you are committed to her, and you are willing to continue to be a part of her life. That may be conveyed in words, whether written or spoken, and can be a note slipped under her door, a letter stuck in her notebook, or a text message sent to her after a couple of hours. There just needs to be some type of affirmation, such as the following:

> *"Sweetheart, I want you to know that your mom and I love you just as much today, knowing what is happening with you, as the day we brought you home into our family."*
> *"Beth, your dad and I are happy that we get to put things on the table and discuss where you are in your relationships."*
> *"Molly, we're not going to stop loving you and want you to know that we will never allow anyone to take you to a place that you really don't want to be."*
> *"Randi, we love you."*

Why would you say these things? Because when any teen is caught or exposed, the greatest fear is that he or she is no longer loved. Saying these things, even if the response is as negative as you can imagine, affirms the relationship. Your daughter needs to hear your affirmations of your relationship, especially as you move through the process of helping her become healthy again.

Expression

A day or two after exposing the issue, it's time to get together and share with your teen what you feel about the same-sex relationship. The comments you make might look similar to these:

> *"Suzie, we want you to know that we're not in favor of this relationship and feel like it's wrong. It's wrong because it will take you to a place where you don't want*

to end up. *The end result of these relationships puts you in a place where you will never walk down the aisle at your wedding for me to give you away. You may never have your own children. Your future family will look so different than what you have always wanted.*"

"*Christina, we can't allow this to happen. It is against what we believe for you, what we want for you, and what we think you want for yourself.*"

"*Amber, you know this isn't right; and we want to help you any way we know how. There is no way that we can be supportive of this relationship.*"

"*Melissa, we love you, and love you enough not to allow you to walk down this path with our support. We will have to stand for what we believe is right.*"

This meeting is a time to express what you feel—and to ask your daughter what she feels. You are bringing your emotions to the table, and hopefully, she'll bring hers. She will know what you are thinking, and hopefully you'll find out what she's thinking (or not thinking). It's from that standpoint that you'll be able to strategize about your next steps.

Let me share with you a couple of thoughts at this point:

When you begin to share your heart with your child, I would encourage you not to use Scripture to back up your claims. Your child has already heard it, because you are already living it. It will only throw gasoline on a raging emotional fire. Scripture can be reflected in your comments without having to quote chapter and verse, and it can be communicated without bombarding her with comments like, "*You know what Scripture says…*" or "*What you are doing is so against God.*" While these may be truthful statements, they may not be appropriate at this time, because what you are trying to do now is to draw your daughter out so that you can have more discussion. This is not the time to shame her or condemn her, which will only drive her back into herself and her own ways. It's learning to speak the truth in love, and in such a way that it leads a person to repentance and restoration, not in a way that drives her away.

Expectations

The third meeting is where you share your expectations for the situation. I would implore you first to seek wisdom either from a counselor, a pastor, or some trusted friend, as the directives you give during this time can be costly. This is the tough discussion where you detail what you are going to do and how you are going to do it. You'll notice the escalating intensity of the message:

> *"Allison, we can't allow this relationship to continue, so we're either going to ask you to control it and stop seeing 'x,' or we'll have to put some controls around you to protect you. We want you to start going to a counselor to talk about all of this just to make sure that you're thinking straight (no pun intended) and not headed in a direction that is going to eventually hurt you."*

> *"Pam, your mom and I can't allow you to go back to the school you've been attending because we feel you can't break away from 'x.' It's almost like she's controlling you, and you can't think on your own."*

> *"Karen, we've tried counseling, taking things away from you, pleading with you, and hoping that things would turn, but it just doesn't seem to be happening. We've decided to have you go to a place where you can be protected and can also receive some help to get through this craziness."*

> *"We love you, Kate. And we love you enough that we don't want you to head down a path that you really don't want to walk. We want you to spend the summer at Aunt Jane's (or at a summer camp working in the kitchen, or on a mission project, or working at a family business) and just take a break from everything."*

> *"Meg, you and I are going to get away for awhile to talk and spend some time thinking through all that's been going on in your life. I want you to plan on being gone a month. This means no cell phones and no contact with anyone back home except Dad and your sisters."*

> *"Mary, we love you. But we don't support what you're doing with 'x,' and if it continues, you'll no longer be able to live at home. You can't ignore our rules, beliefs, and*

principles. You're 17, and we can't make you do what you don't want to do, but we won't support this. As long as it continues, we will not support you at college. We won't pay for college, and we won't be giving you money. You'll be on your own. The ball is in your court. This would not be our choice; it is your choice if you cannot do what we ask of you while you're in our home. We can't support your lifestyle, as your choices will only lead you to ruin, and we won't be part of that. We love you too much."

In the above examples, parents are clearly stating what they will do and won't do. You can tell from the intensity of the subject matter and severity of the consequences why I would encourage and almost demand that you seek counsel before implementing any of them. I always suggest a strong response, as I truly believe that this situation demands one. But when you pose a strong response to your daughter's actions, be ready for a strong reaction. Not knowing all the details of your situation, it's hard to give complete guidance. That is why I state the necessity of talking with someone who is familiar with your situation and can speak wisdom into your specific circumstances.

No matter what measures you have to take, at no time do you completely cut off your child. You just refuse to support what she is doing. You can still have her over for dinner, invite your child for Thanksgiving and any birthdays. It's just that she won't receive your full support while she continues to live a lifestyle that you are in disagreement with. If your daughter decides to leave home and live with her girlfriend, you can still have her over and require that the significant other not come.

During this time, I would also encourage you to engage your friends, your daughter's friends, and any other person who has been important in your daughter's life to invite your child for a cup of coffee or lunch—so that your teen has other people who can speak wisdom into her life. Your teen may share with and listen to family members and close friends in a way that she won't with you. Friends and family members can also reiterate how much they want your teen to make better choices. It also gets the situation fully "out of the closet" so that your teen has nowhere else to hide.

Parents ask me how long it will take for the child to "turn around." Honestly, I have no idea. It could be one day; it could be ten years. The intent is that as long as your child is "on your watch," you will make sure that you're providing every opportunity for your daughter to make healthy decisions and are doing everything you can to get her to think through her choices and walk in the manner that she truly believes.

At some point, your daughter will be able to live on her own without your support, and she can make any choices she wants without your blessing or agreement. If that is the case, you might have to learn to act with love towards your daughter in the midst of her sin, knowing that you are doing everything possible to help her come back to a good place in her life.

My encouragement to you is to love her strongly during the time that she is being negatively influenced, and to love her the hard way by allowing her to come to some conclusions about her own life.

QUESTION 4

What If My Teen's
Friends Are Bad News?

*"What do you do when your teenager starts
associating with a peer group that you know is
very bad news? Their language is bad, and they are
smoking, drinking, doing drugs, and sexually active.
The problem is that this group's parents are much the
same. We see that our teen is starting to participate in
a progressive way. Should we work to prevent contact,
move to another city, or be heavy-handed in our
dealings with our daughter?"*

It begins the first day you send your children to school. Within
a week they may come home and tell you that there isn't a Santa
Claus. Not very long after, they utter the word "stupid," tell you
to "shut up" for the first time, and share a new vocabulary word
that depicts a hot place and rhymes with "smell." As you see your
child's innocence flying out the window, you might begin to feel
that the "other kids" at school have taken something from your
child that you weren't quite ready to relinquish. The challenge
of peer pressure, outside influence, and exposure begins. From
kindergarten until now, you have found that the influence of
other kids on your kids, at times, pushes them in a direction that
you would rather not go and forces you to have to counterpunch
the effect and influence. You also have to spend a lot more time
explaining why you would rather not have your child doing what
others are doing.

One of the greatest challenges of parenting is balancing when to protect and when to expose. There's not one of us who doesn't want to protect our children from influences that would take them to a place we'd prefer they not go. If you had control over your children their whole lives, protecting them forever would be a great and honorable goal. But the truth is, one day you will relinquish control, allow them to make their own decisions, and they will leave the comforts of your home and enter a world that they must live in.

The challenge of protecting vs. exposing is all in the timing. We hate when our cute little child finds out there isn't a Santa Claus, but we all know that having a 16-year-old who still believes in Ol' St. Nick is just a little weird. Somewhere in between that cute and weird time, exposure will happen and innocence will leave. The intent and goal of a parent must move from protection to preparation. Sadly, many parents spend too much time focused on the former and not enough on the latter.

Parents should be training their child for the world that they *will* eventually live in and not the more ideal world that the parents *think* they should live in. Let me give you an example: If our military, which engages in battle on a daily basis, was only trained in jungle warfare, I'm sure that casualties would be slightly higher if the battle at hand was in the desert. And if military command only trained for battle in the desert, then there would be trouble if they had to fight in the mountains. I hope that you understand my point. It is essential that parents understand where their children will be and what they will face in their life, so that the appropriate tasks will be learned.

One day, your child will date. Your precious baby—now a teen—will be exposed to smoking, drinking, drugs, and sexually active friends. He will drive a car. He may become a parent. She will probably be a wife or he will be a husband. Your teens will live in society. They will engage in debate. They will be around people who do not believe like they do. They will be confronted about what they believe. They will experience tragedy. They will need to get themselves out of bed on their own. They will one day work at a job. They will make mistakes. And they will make poor choices. Are you training them for these "engagements," these ongoing "battles"?

If you are training your children as you are encouraged to do so in scripture (Proverbs 22:6, NIV, says, *"Train a child in the way he should go..."*), then I would ask: What you are training them for?

That's an important question, because if you don't know where you're going, then any road will lead you there. The goals you set for training will help you respond to the question of "How do I respond?" when difficult situations are laid at your doorstep. Here's an example: *How should I respond to the issues of bad language, smoking, drinking, drugs, and sexual activity?* I'm sure that the world your children will eventually move into upon graduation from high school, if they're not there already, will be a world full of bad language, smoking, drinking, drugs, and sexual activity. If your teen is 13, I'd give you one answer. If she is 16, I'd give you another. And you'll get a completely different answer if he is 18. And all of those various answers depend on the intention of your training.

So what are the goals of your training?

Protection and Overprotection

God has called you to protect your kids. Anything short of protection can be sometimes labeled as neglect. It's an instinctive response to any potential danger that your child may face. If you didn't feel a need to protect, you wouldn't be a good mother or father. There are times when you protect by defending your teen, insuring that injustice and malice doesn't come his way. This is done by the way that you set up your home, develop your rules and consequences, and set your boundaries. Then there are times that you protect by being proactive when someone tries to damage your child. At times, you protect your teens by not allowing them to hurt themselves. And of course, there are other times when you allow some things to happen in the life of your teen to prepare her for what is to come. In all these ways, you are protecting your kids.

Overprotection can postpone, delay, or prevent the training your child needs because of your unwillingness to allow anything to happen that might cause discomfort, pain, or hurt. Most of the time, overprotection is fear-based; parents are fearful of something or some person and what might happen if their child associates with that thing or person.

Not allowing your third grader to go outside to play because she might skin her knee could be overprotection. Not allowing your child to ride a horse because you were thrown off of a horse when you were a child might be overprotection. Not allowing your child to watch TV, get on the computer, or watch movies might be overprotection. Keeping your child from playing video games might be overprotection.

I can't tell you what overprotection looks like for your family. Everyone knows that it exists, and most people see it in other families but can't see it in their own. The purpose of me bringing it up here is simple: Parents are supposed to protect their children, but not to the point that they are prevented from receiving some necessary exposure and experiences that will train them to be able to handle and make good choices in the upcoming world they are to live in.

There's a young man I know that, through the good intentions of his parents, was homeschooled through the tenth grade. It was the type of homeschooling that had minimal social interaction with other kids, kept the young man with his mother most of the day, and didn't allow him to experience normal activities unless there was an educational purpose for the activities. His parents then thought it would be a good idea to put him in high school to let him experience social activity and learn to engage with people. His sophomore year was a disaster. He couldn't function, didn't know how to relate to people, was awkward in his conversation, and would then try what I would call "stupid stunts" to get the attention of his fellow classmates in an attempt to win their acceptance. He finished his sophomore year labeled as a "dork," shamed by girls around him, ridiculed by his peers, friendless, and withdrawn into depression. He was so "marked" that his parents sent him to live with friends in another state so he would have, at least, exposure to some family other than his own.

His father stated to me that what happened to his son was a prime example of why he hated the world, and that he never should have put his child in the public school. He accused every teacher and school administrator of not providing a safe environment for his son. He pointed the finger at everyone except himself. When I think of this man and his wife, after watching what happened to their son, I think of the scripture that states, *"The way of a fool seems right to him..."* (Proverbs 12:15 NIV).

That father called me one day and asked me what I thought. The Scripture, *"Even a fools is thought wise if he keeps silent, and discerning if he holds his tongue."* (Proverbs 17:28 NIV) flashed through my head. But call me a fool, I couldn't resist. I shared my thoughts and told him how I thought that he was well-intentioned in what he had done with his son, but so overprotective that he had missed the opportunity to train his child to be able to function in the world in which he would eventually have to live.

His overprotection had kept the concept of "iron sharpens iron" from happening in the life of his son. His son buckled under pressure because he had never experienced any. He didn't know how to take ridicule, criticism, and meanness from his peers. He didn't know how to be less than the best in his class. He had always been at the top of his class, because he was the only one in his class through his first 10 years of school! He didn't know how to socially engage because he had never been around any girls in a social setting, and he had never really developed any close friends other than study buddies.

Have a plan for training. Protect your child. But don't overprotect to the point that your children don't experience what they need to. Kids need to learn some great lessons necessary to function as adults in this world.

So What If the Friends Really Are Bad News?

I'll answer it using another proverb about fools. *"He who walks with the wise grows wise, but a companion of fools suffers harm."* (Proverbs 13:20, NIV) and another scripture from Romans, *"Not only so, but we also rejoice in our sufferings, because we know that suffering produces perseverance; perseverance, character and character, hope."* (Romans 5:3-4, NIV).

Somewhere in the mix of both these Scriptures lies my answer. I would encourage parents to allow exposure into the life of their teen to the point that it can be used for training and developing some great character qualities, but never to the point that a teen would suffer damage or harm. Allow the experiences to hurt at times, but never to the point of causing lasting damage.

Should you allow your child to hang around people who are using bad language, smoking, drinking, using drugs and being sexually active? I would give an answer based upon the age of your teen.

If your teen is 13 years old and hanging around these kids, I would get your child away as soon as possible. Your teen is probably young enough to continue to listen to the voice of reason and would understand your concern. Chances are it is something "new" to your teen, and these behaviors are new as well. To what extent would I remove my child? I would switch schools if need be. This is pretty abnormal behavior for kids that young, and if parents are fueling this type of inappropriate behavior, it's only going to get worse. I would report these parents to the police, report the other kids to school authorities, and limit your child's hang-time with these kids.

If your teen is 16 years old, sadly, this behavior is more common. I would make sure that you and your teen are talking and spending some time using this as a discussion moment of teaching. In these discussions, you could share your thoughts about your teen's involvement and what you would do if the behavior continues. I would make the statement, *"I can't allow you to be with these friends, and if it doesn't stop, we'll have to look at some alternative schools, alternative living arrangements, and some structure that will provide you the framework to make better choices. I can't allow this to continue."*

At this point, I would make sure that there are external controls put in place around those areas where your teen has shown he either has not developed his own internal controls or is choosing not to use them. Take away the car keys, cell phone, insurance, activities (when needed), and ground when necessary. You must work to prevent anything further from happening.

If your teen is 18, there's not a whole lot that you can do to limit her involvement with these friends. But you can make sure that you're having discussions about why you disagree with her choices and why it is of concern to you. There's really not much you can do except try to appeal to your teen and help her understand that the behavior she is engaged in will only take her to a place where you're not sure she wants to end up. If your teen is under your roof, you do have the right to tell her that she cannot continue to live there if she cannot abide by your rules. Again, don't cut off all ties with your child; let your teens know they are loved and welcome to visit. But they can't live there unless they can live with your standards.

You must make decisions for and with your child so that in the future, you can look back and have no regrets about the actions that you took. It may be better to do too much and be able to back off should you find that you're being a little strict, than to do too little and have to add more restrictions when situations begin to spin out of control. It's a lot easier to ease up than it is to tighten the reins when needed.

Spend Some Time Together

Most parents don't spend time with their child in discussion until there is something wrong and communication is needed. If lines of communication are not established before a conflict, then the crisis requires two actions rather just one – first, establishing the lines of communication and then actually communicating. The ounce of prevention here is making sure that you spend time with your child on a regular basis, chatting and discussing life in times of nonconflict, so that you have a basis from which to start when issues arise.

This is my most highly recommended counsel, and I've got to tell you, the least followed advice. For whatever reason, people don't seem to spend regular time with their children having discussions. Those habits are good habits to have in place when bad things begin to happen.

Those Bad Kids

I've lived with "those bad kids" for more than 30 years. What I've found is that they're all really good kids who are just making some really poor choices. Poor, because their actions will take them to a place where they don't want to end up. "Bad kids" are just kids making decisions without any wisdom—either because they ignored it or it wasn't offered to them. They're simply acting foolish. And because kids hang out together, there are always other kids who are influenced to participate. When opportunity knocks, teens open the door.

There is a tendency to blame a child's actions on the influence of those other "bad kids," but you should never excuse your child's behavior as just that. Your child has chosen what he's done for a reason. When you excuse his behavior and blame others, you miss what's really happening in the heart and mind of your teen. You miss the root issues. And your teen may get lost in the process. Too many times, what parents think of as bad influences, teens look at as good opportunities.

QUESTION 5

What do I do If My Son Has Been "Porn" Again?

"I recently walked in on my son while he was engrossed in a sex video on the Internet. We have suspected other times that he's been looking at porn. I don't know whether he's just curious or addicted. I fear that this is giving him the wrong perception about girls around him and could lead him down a path that could damage him. My husband says it's not that big of a deal; that 'All young guys take a peek now and then,' and I do remember my husband looking at magazines when we were first married. Any advice?"

The positive side of the Internet is that it has opened the world to new information, new communication, and new ways of purchasing items. The negative side of the Internet is the availability of pornography (and gambling) at the click of a button. The porn industry has become a billion-dollar one that provides many ways for anyone to find nude and erotic pictures of men and women without much trying. It's nothing new. The porn industry has been around since the beginning of painting and photography, but the Internet has magnified it because of the immediate access for everyone.

Today's teens are the first generation to live when porn has been readily available and easily accessible all the time—often, in the privacy of their own rooms. Our teens, during a time in their lives when they are naturally curious about sex, can see it live, raw, and unfiltered at the click of a mouse. It's affecting teens deeply, and it is rapidly changing the image young men today have of girls and what they expect from them. It's also affecting the girls, but more on that later.

Your Son

Let me focus on the guys first. Bottom line: If you have a teenage son, and he's on the Internet without filters to block porn sites, he's already looked at sites that are inappropriate. I don't know of one guy who hasn't. I'm convinced that most guys would "take a peek" if given the chance. You know why? They're wired that way. God has made men to be visual people. And God has put in the heart of every man a longing to look at the nakedness of the most beautiful of His creation, woman. It's a great desire that I applaud and am thankful for. I'm happy for those young men who want to see a naked woman. In the same breath, I would add that I want those desires that young men experience to be limited to viewing only the naked body of the woman they are married to, their wife, the woman they are committed to for life.

No teen (or adult, for that matter) is justified in searching the Web for pictures of naked men and women or videos of sex acts. There is nothing in Christianity that gives license to a young man to pursue such actions, even because he is just curious. However, knowing that God created them to be curious does help us understand why guys search and look.

Thus, the problem is not that there is a desire to look. The problem is the availability of porn. Even the best computer filters, spam guards, and Internet security systems cannot keep all images from coming to your child when he searches the Internet.

If your son has a computer in his room, I could tell you what he has most likely looked at or searched for. You wouldn't put a *Playboy* magazine in your son's room and truly believe that he wouldn't ever look at it, would you? My answer to the question of whether to put a private computer in your son's room is: *"Absolutely Not!"* Put the computer in a room where the screen faces a direction that allows others to see what he is looking at (I'll mention other monitoring devices and procedures later). If it's already in there, take it out of the bedroom and put it in a family room where accountability comes in the form of the presence of other people. This new way of thinking may bring about changes in the placement of computers within your home and how you monitor wireless Internet access.

But what if you do catch your son on the Internet looking at porn? Let me suggest a few things that I have found to be true:

An understanding of your son's raging hormones, the sexual nature of today's culture, and the availability of pornographic material online should cause you to be forewarned about the possibility—no, the probability—that your child has or will view porn online. Hopefully, that knowledge will calm your response when you confirm that he has.

Another thing I have found helpful is that if Dad is in the picture, let Dad handle it. Men are wired the same, and it's just one of those things that I don't think Moms understand too well. Dad, let your son know that it's inappropriate and it's got to stop. Be very clear that if it doesn't, your teen will lose the computer because he can't be responsible and honor your request. Of course, your son is going to ask you if you ever looked at any *Playboy* when you were his age. You can tell him that you did, but it doesn't make it right and it isn't right today.

As a matter of fact, because it was harder to get in the past, porn was much less of an issue back then. The greater problem now is that porn is so readily acceptable, so explicit, and in such unlimited abundance. Because of these factors, there is a much greater threat of addiction, dependency, and influence than in the past. Ask any man. Reuters reported on October 18, 2006, that Internet addiction has now become a quantifiable problem affecting one in eight U.S. adults, according to a Stanford University of Medicine study. [1]

With all the sexual bombardment of today's culture, finding a son looking at porn on the Internet is not the end of the world, nor is it the end of his innocence. So please don't treat it as such. Treat a first-time offense as just that—a first-time offense. I've seen too many young people dead set on violating their parents' directives, not because they don't agree with their parents' observations and beliefs, but because of the way the parents handle their molehill and turn it into a mountain.

If your son continues his actions, and those actions move quickly into a habit, further action on the part of the parents must be taken. Get rid of the computer. Poke his eyes out (Just kidding!). Take something else away: the car, the insurance to the car, one wheel and tire from the car, or the cell phone. Do something. Something that will make your teen uncomfortable. Don't just sit back and allow your child to dive headfirst into a very deep "shallow place" on the Internet. Not all people who look at porn are addicted; but those who are started with a peek.

Your Daughter

Now, it's the girls' turn. Let me address the effect that Internet porn is having on them. They're not as likely to be viewing porn as the guys, but the fact that the guys around them are looking at these images—and believe me, the girls know it—creates a harder world for teen girls to live in.

Today's teen girls live in a world of sexual innuendo and an atmosphere of seduction, where presentation is important and their definition of modesty has changed. It's changed not so much because of the lack of values taught by parents, but because of the overwhelming amount of media (TV, internet, movies, magazines, and radio) exposure given to various and different lifestyles. The media has overwhelmed girls with images and suggestions that what once was taboo is now acceptable. Quite honestly, we've all been affected by this.

Girls Gone Wild videos give a new definition of what is acceptable and not acceptable on the beach and at parties. Girls flashing breasts at Mardi Gras to get krewe members on floats to throw beads has moved from unacceptable to normal. Victoria's Secret (where there are no secrets) displays lingerie that never used to be displayed. The chatter among teens about menstrual cycles, body parts, erectile dysfunction and the newest type of tampons is now acceptable discussion.

Life has changed, and it's not just because of the Internet. It's just that the Internet is, in part, a way to expose new ideas, thoughts, images, and lifestyles. The Internet has brought a new medium of communication to the lives of our kids, exposing them to the once-unexposed. Our daughters and granddaughters get stuck in the middle of trying to live in a way that parents have taught and live what's acceptable in social settings. It's a tough spot to be in.

Girls are given messages throughout the electronic and digital world that if you don't present yourself as sexy, you won't get noticed. It's a culture of fear that is fueled by messages of permission that say it is okay to show more skin than what you have been taught is okay. I don't think parents quite understand the tremendous amount of pressure this places on a child. Girls that I have been associated with are torn between doing what is socially acceptable and what is required by their families and church. Unless people can sit down and discuss this issue, more times than not, the social pressure will win out. Thus, girls who have grown up in the church and have great parents then present themselves in ways that are not in line with the values they have learned. And it's all because of their deep longing to be noticed, to be valued, and to socially "fit."

So porn does affect girls, even if they are not looking at it. Very few teen girls that I know or have met actually surf the net looking for porn. But most have been on the Internet long enough to know that the massive bombardment of images has changed their definition of what is now acceptable and what is not. That's the first way girls are affected. This lowering of the standard is fueled by their male counterparts' encouragement to do "what everyone else is doing." This creates a perfect storm that places parents in the awkward position of wanting to allow their teen daughter to be stylish and wanting her to be modest at the same time.

Appearance is a big thing in the minds of most teen girls. And porn has raised many young men's expectations of what they want from girls or expect them to show. When guys' expectations are raised, and girls' modesty level is lowered, I would submit to you that there is a much greater chance of your teenage daughter getting hurt. Our girls are falling quickly into experiences that can destroy their lives.

I hear moms and dads all over the country express great frustration over how to help their daughter live modestly in a seductive, visually oriented, and digitally bombarded world. The answer to their question is always that they have to do something, rather than nothing. Parameters must be set, communicated, and adhered to. And it must be a set of parameters that is revisited and discussed often.

QUESTION

What If My Teen Is Having Sex?

"We know our 16-year-old son is having sex with his girlfriend, and we're not sure how to approach the subject with him or her. We've talked to her parents, and they are just as confused as we are and just as much at a loss. We never expected this, and now we wonder about issues of birth control, curfew, their relationship, and potential pregnancy. We're spinning! Can you give us (and her parents) some direction?"

"We found a disturbing letter in my daughter's book bag directed to her boyfriend (that we did not know she had). I'm afraid she's already having sex. I would like to do anything in my power to prevent her from becoming pregnant. We try to talk to her, but she refuses to speak the truth about the current situation. She is an honor student, but we feel she is very influenced by her peers. We found out she has been skipping classes, more than likely to be with him. She's a Christian girl who's never given us a bit of trouble. Should we just leave it alone and let it pass?"

A friend of mine recently sent me an e-mail that quoted an anonymous "Senility Prayer." It's a take-off of the Alcoholics Anonymous "Serenity Prayer," and it made me chuckle. Here's how it goes:

"Lord, grant me the senility to forget the people I never liked anyway, the good fortune to run into the ones I do like, and the eyesight to tell the difference."

My friend always sends me things to remind me that I'm getting older. It's good that he does. His little funny blurbs to me, mostly about aging, remind me that I am changing and that change is inevitable. And if I am changing, so is the world around me. The truth is that every year I continue to work with teens, I find that they're getting younger and younger. I also find out that there are some things that I cannot change about today's teen culture. Here's the real "Serenity Prayer":

"God, give us grace to accept with serenity the things that cannot be changed, courage to change the things that should be changed, and the wisdom to distinguish the one from the other." [1]

I know that I'm never going to be able to change the sexual culture that our teens are growing up in. I wish I could, for I see the heartbreak and struggles that teens go through as a result of the influence of this highly sexual society.

Since the beginning of mankind, sex issues have surrounded cultures and relationships, and teens have always struggled. I was no exception. I'm sure that there weren't many ninth grade kids as horny as I was, nor anyone who wanted to look at a *Playboy* magazine more than I did. Sex dominated my conversations and thoughts while I was involved in youth group, even after I became a Christian, and when I was the Oklahoma Bible Quiz Champ of 1969. I was a virgin when I got married, but I'm not so sure I really wanted to be.

The morals and principles of my girlfriend (later to be my wife) pushed her to fight off the advances that I brought her way. Plus, her mother kept bugging us whenever we came home from a date by flashing the outdoor lights on and off so much that it was rather distracting. (I think that was her intent.) I really thought that if I ever touched my girlfriend and her dad found out about it, he would kill me. I further knew, beyond the shadow of a doubt, that if I ever had sex with anyone, God would no longer like me. This was a true belief because it was what I was taught by a well-meaning Sunday school teacher. I also knew that if I got anyone pregnant, the girl would be sent off to a concentration camp, taken to Mexico for an abortion, or moved to a faraway land to live with relatives.

The message communicated to me loud and clear was that if I really liked a girl, I'd better treat her like a gentleman or I would lose her. And the overall message from our culture was that you "sleep with the one you're married to, and keep your pants zipped up until you have a ring on your finger." In some mighty way, every one of these influences worked together to keep me on the straight and narrow. I have a feeling that many of you are laughing, having experienced the same thing.

Things have changed a little, haven't they? No, they've changed a lot. Exposure to so much sexual stuff in this culture has done a couple of things to teens today. And wanting to limit my thoughts to just a couple of areas to complete a chapter and not write a whole book about the subject, I would share with you the two areas of concern that I think are invasive now in teen culture. These are permissiveness and prevalence.

Permissiveness

Our society has truly given permission for our teens, and just about anybody, to be more sexually involved with one another than any past generation. Teens do understand and welcome (most of the time) their parents' messages about values, abstinence, and premarital sex. But the overwhelming and gargantuan influence of the culture has a tendency to dwarf the positive message that parents so diligently want their teens to hear.

I haven't met a mom or dad yet who is really comfortable with their teen having sex with someone. There just aren't too many moms and dads, Republican or Democrat, liberal or conservative, Jew or Gentile, or Texan or non-Texan that really believe, in their heart of hearts, that they are "okay" with their son or daughter shacking up before the child gets married. I know parents would prefer their children wait, hold off, exercise self-constraint, and keep themselves for their future spouses. If parents did not want their teens to abstain, they would only encourage their teens' sexual activity and make adolescence nothing more than a glamorized orgy. I have yet to meet any parent who desires this.

The permission for sexual activity that teens get today is not from their parents. It is from the culture through its example and display. Where do teens find this example? Look at the top celebrities. All teens have to do is read or hear about the lives of famous people they admire. Or they can surf the Internet and get exposed to a world of sexually graphic display and discussion. They can turn on the TV or hit the movies, read *Seventeen* or *Cosmo Girl* magazines. They get permission from the world of sensual style and glamor and through the changing laws that allow vulgarity and obscenity, through the examples of fallen preachers and politicians and by hearing about fellow students having sex with teachers. They find permission in the applauding of sports heroes and their exploitations, in the intrigue of videos, and the fascination of fantasy depictions. They see sexual permissiveness in reality shows that are sometimes too real, and the list can go on and on. Permission is given everywhere, in a society that encourages teens to "go for" what they want—right now.

Here's the second area of concern: We're surrounded.

Prevalence

It's everywhere, isn't it? It's gotten to the point that I don't even blush anymore when I hear certain words or see certain images. I am more tolerant of things that I didn't think I'd ever be tolerant of. I watch movies that I never would have watched years ago. I watch TV shows that never would have been allowed on the air back in my day, and I sit through commercials that discuss things that should never be discussed in public, much less in "mixed company." (What's that, anyway?) This culture has affected me. Has it affected you? I think it has impacted all of us. And, like it or not, it has definitely affected our teens.

The real problem that we face as parents is not just that this seductive culture has given permission for so many things to be different in the lives of our teens, it's that it is so prevalent and present in our lives as well. The whole mess makes me feel like I'm on a beach holding a small bucket in my hand trying to stop the crashing destruction of a tsunami wave that is about to pound on my family with a devastating flood of change. I feel like a "David" standing up against a giant that is one hundred times bigger than I ever could have imagined, with great doubt that I can affect the outcome.

Your teen's world is different from the world we knew and embraced. I'm sure that "horniness" is just as prevalent today as it was in my generation and in many generations previous. But it has never been fueled quite as much as it is today with instant access to pornography, the display of sexual exploits, and the absence of extinguishers that used to keep those hormones and desires in check and in line.

I'm also sure that the "speed limits" that were placed around me, for the most part aren't there today. A moral and principled woman is hard to find. Mothers don't flick the lights as much as they used to. Dads really won't kill a young man who is having sex with their daughters, because now the young men have rights that can't be violated. The message has been sent that God will love you no matter what you do. And if you get pregnant, it's not as big of a deal anymore to keep the baby or give it up for adoption. Not only are girls not sent away in shame anymore if they get pregnant, but also today many high schools have daycare centers for the babies of the students! Waiting until marriage to have sex just doesn't hold as much water as it used to.

Allow me to ask some questions: Did you think that your teen would not be influenced by the sexual environment they live in? Did you think that the pressure wouldn't touch her? How I wish it wouldn't. But I know that it does. And I'm convinced that while we can't change the tide of the sexual nature of our culture, we can battle it with what we have—the influence we have over our child. And that's a lot bigger than a bucket, even when it doesn't seem like it.

If every parent, including you, did what he or she could to influence teens, then you wouldn't have to worry about the culture. Your positive influence will help your child navigate through the poor choices he makes, the mistakes she talks to you about, the lifestyle he lives, and the never-ending ways she shocks you.

This culture is tough on our sons and daughters. I know few parents who would choose to grow up in this day and time. To think that your teens won't be influenced by this tough, sexually-charged culture is faulty thought.

So if that means that you have now found out they're having sex with their boyfriends and girlfriends, I would share with you some things I've learned through the years of living with hundreds of kids who have engaged in sexual activity long before any parents would have desired for them to do so.

Your Daughter

There's no doubt in my mind that the sexual nature of this teen culture creates more pressure, thus more difficulties, for our girls. Pornography; the display of sexual activity in media; the sexually connotative themes throughout literature, magazines, and advertising; and the presentation and exposure of alternative sexual lifestyles, coupled with a message of instant gratification and a "Do what you want" mentality, set young girls up for a fall. Your daughter is under severe pressure, the type of pressure that you wouldn't wish on yourself. So, when she falls, it is of utmost importance that you know how to approach the subject and discuss the pitfalls of premarital sex.

When you find out that your daughter is having sex with someone, there's no question that it is a devastating realization. I encourage you to take a couple of steps back, and don't respond with your first inclination. Your first swing may work well in golf, but it doesn't work in an emotionally charged, disappointing situation. Let things sit for a night, even if you catch your daughter in the act. Gather your thoughts, think through what you want to say, and seek counsel from someone you trust. Just having someone else hear your thoughts and respond to your emotions with a sense of wit and wisdom is always helpful.

When a daughter becomes sexually active, most parents look at their teen's actions as a loss of something (i.e. virginity, innocence, purity, or childhood). While parents may see it as a loss, a teen may not feel that way. She may believe she's gained something in a relationship that she would not have had otherwise if she had not become sexually active (i.e. a new relationship, new experience, new level of commitment, womanhood). The friction between the parents' sense of loss and the teen's sense of gain may cause so much heat that relationships are burned, and a once-loving dynamic goes down in flames. Hopefully, this warning will further emphasize the need for you to walk gently toward your daughter when you find out that she has been having sex. A parent's approach is crucial during this time. And going in with a hail of gunfire is not usually an effective strategy.

Once your teen has had that first sexual experience, her mind-set changes. I'm not sure how to describe it other than it's just different. She now "knows" something different, she's violated something special, and she now engages in conversation differently than before her enlightenment. This is why parents are sometimes baffled at why their "b.s." (before sex) teen, who once was so loving in conversation, is now "a.s." (after sex) so arrogant, adamant, and disrespectful. She might make comments like, "You can't tell me what to do with my body" or "I don't believe 'that' anymore" or "You can't stop me" or "I won't get pregnant," or "It's not that big of a deal!"

It's just different, because your teen is different.

I wish I could tell you some magical or special words that would solve this new problem. Truth is, parents can't really stop it. I believe that there are more controls that can be put into place (especially the younger a daughter is), but at best, short of locking up a teen (most parents' first thought), it is not an action that can always be controlled. I'm not saying you then just ignore the issue and not address it. And I'm not saying that you should give permission to your daughter to continue in her behavior just because I'm saying that it's hard to control. I am saying that it's a tough row to hoe, and finding a solution is not always successful or easy.

I'm going to use some cutoff ages as reference points. Keep in mind that these are just guidelines and can be fluid. I use the age of 16 as that age of demarcation that divides the time before which parents may have some influence and control over their teen's choices, and that age span afterward where there is little that can be done. The reason I choose 16 is that it is usually the time when teens receive the privileges of newfound freedoms such as jobs, driving a car, and dating. All three of these items accentuate the fact that parents are losing more and more control over their teens as their teens assume more and more responsibilities outside the home and enlarge their circle of roaming.

If your daughter is under 16, chances are her sexual activity is experimental, fueled by foolish choices, or she's being taken advantage of by a guy who has "staked a claim" to your daughter and intends to "set up shop." These trysts are usually just a passing thing for the young man, but with potentially lifelong damage to your daughter, who has been conned into thinking that her sexual expressions are a relational style that will bring her that attention she wants and the companionship she desires.

Some control mechanisms that can be easily enforced for teens under 16 are a change of schools, a restraining order against the fellow she's hooked up with, a decision to homeschool, enrolling her in a nunnery (I'm half kidding, half not), sending her to relatives to get her away from the negative influence, or the taking away of privileges. Her attitude toward having sex and her response to you after being discovered should be some the deciding factors as to whether or not you enforce extreme consequences, such as having her removed from the home and sent to live elsewhere.

For girls who are over 16, parents can use all the same tactics, but short of placing a child in a structured and monitored environment, there just isn't an easy answer to the question of how a parent gets a child to stop. Parents can put up roadblocks, making sexual activity harder, but most times, teens will find their way around the pylons. Roadblocks could be the taking away of a car, earlier curfews, rules about who can come over to the house, and "flicking the lights" just about every way you know how.

If you have a teen who is sexually active, the discussion of birth control will more than likely come up. If it doesn't and you know that your child is active, then I would encourage you to bring it to the table. This is a touchy discussion among many people who believe that distributing birth control gives license for teens to be sexually active. In the cases of all the kids that I have dealt with, I have not found that to be true. What I hear most parents say who have faced the challenge of an unmarried pregnant daughter is that they wish they would have encouraged birth control.

I don't believe the distribution of condoms and birth control pills encourages sexual activity anymore than putting up a speed limit sign encourages people to drive faster. It would be an easier position otherwise if I saw it to be true. I just don't, and I have dealt with hundreds of families in this situation.

Don't Shame Your Daughter

I believe in abstinence programs. I believe in holding high standards for our teens and helping them attain God's best for their lives. I believe in making commitments and sticking with them. I believe that it is good for a dad to get his daughter to pledge to him that she will keep herself for her future husband.

Sadly, there are times when we hold the standards so high that, if teens fall or make a mistake, they feel like their actions are unforgivable, and they're out of favor because of a poor choice. I love programs that encourage great things for teens and help them wade through the tumultuous waters of adolescence. I hate programs that shame teens when they stumble and don't meet that high standard. I read from a 2003 Northern Kentucky University study that as many as 60 percent of teens who pledge to remain faithful to their future husband or wife don't hold to their commitment.[2] I see this issue as an area where we lose so many teens from the church, from the fellowship, and from our community. Shame on us for shaming them!

God assures each one of us of His presence always. He doesn't leave us when we make a mistake, nor does He turn his back on His children when they sin. He doesn't disappear when the road gets dark, nor does He abandon us during a time of need. He moves *toward* us in hopes of restoration, forgiveness, and reconciliation. I would encourage all parents to do likewise when faced with a teen who has fallen into sexual sin. It does no good to shame anyone. Do you respond well when someone embarrasses you? There should be consequences for sinful and inappropriate behavior, you bet. But you should never demean. That approach only destroys relationships and builds walls of resentment. This is not the time to be burning bridges (Remember the friction between your loss and their gain?) that will have to be crossed in the future. Your daughter needs you now, and she will need you ten years from now, when what is happening now will be long gone.

It's easy to love teens when they're doing well. It's harder to love them when they're struggling and making mistakes. But that may be the time when they need it most. I guess what it comes down to for parents is this: Can you still love your daughter if she is sexually active? She needs you to love her, no matter what. If she doesn't feel certain of your love in every circumstance, it could be one of the reasons that she is sexually active. She may be looking for a love that is less conditional than the love she feels from you only when she is a "good girl."

Let me put this in perspective. I don't believe, as Scripture would support, that it's right for anyone to have premarital sex. I think it jumbles up relationships and causes damage that could hurt a teen's future marriage. But in my experience with teens, there are a lot worse things than finding out your daughter is sexually active.

Many would ask why I don't mention sexually transmitted diseases when I talk about teen promiscuity. That's because I don't think the discussion of diseases or the dissemination of material about them is a deterrent to sexual activity. I think that discussion is about as effective as my dermatologist telling me to stay out of the sun, my cardiologist telling me to not eat potato chips, and a highway patrolman telling me to wear my seat belt. It might encourage a teen to think about the use of condoms, but it doesn't seem to deter sexual promiscuity.

What If Your Daughter Is Pregnant?

If you ever hear that news, let me assure you of something. You will get through it, and God will honor His word to cause all things to work together for good. I've seen what many would think is the worst situation turn into the most wonderful of opportunities. And I've got to tell you…hearts turn, a teen matures in ways she never would have matured otherwise, and parents embrace their relationship with their daughter in ways they never would have thought possible.

If you hear this news from your daughter, one of your main concerns should be the health of that unborn child. That means your daughter has to be healthy, and I would stop at nothing to insure that she gets healthy. Help her get the vitamins she needs, to make the right food choices, and to stop the use of any harmful substances (alcohol, drugs, birth control pills, tobacco, even caffeine).

While you are helping your daughter care for herself physically, you will also have some decisions to make. Your daughter will have to decide whether to keep the child or give it up for adoption. Should she choose to place her child for adoption, there are plenty of reputable Christian adoption agencies and attorneys who can help.

For parents, one of the decisions to be made is what their role will be if adoption is not the choice their daughter makes. There are many questions that surround unplanned pregnancies, and there's no way I can answer them all, but out of my experience with teens and their families I will address one issue that is essential to be considered. That issue has to do with your roles as now, new grandparents in the life of this new grandchild.

The first usual response that most new grandparents experience is one of shock and perhaps fears of the unknown. Being surprised by a sudden turn of events in your life and the life of your child is normal as being surprised by any other unexpected events in your life. But this one is far different in nature in that it involves the life a newborn, helpless, and innocent child. Your child may decide to raise her child. She may decide to give her up for adoption. She may ask if you would be involved in the raising in the child. I pray that she will choose those I mention and not the route that many take to terminate the pregnancy.

I've seen many parents, now grandparents, chose, with their daughter, one of the many different options. And I've seen many different results from each of their choices. My encouragement to all new grandparents-to-be is to consider your choices wisely, with counsel from some good and godly friends. Too many times, I see decisions that are acted upon quickly and regretted for years.

I know that in my own life I sometimes interpret "surprises" as distractions from my own plans that I have for my life, so I try to "solve the inconvenience" as quickly as possible, so that I can "get on" with my plans. In the midst of pursuing what I wanted, I mistakenly rejected what God wanted. In hindsight, how I wish I would have sought counsel and spent much more time on my knees seeking His direction, than following my first reaction to pursue "my plan", and quickly by-passing "His plan."

God may be calling you to intervene in the life of this new child. Chances are, you might be in a better position than your daughter to give the child what he or she might need right now. Don't discount the value of what God might be doing in your life. Similarly, God's plan may be for this new baby to enter a new family through adoption. Many "new grandparents" have told me that allowing a daughter to give up a child for adoption is like a death in the family. The magnitude of either decision will change lives in some way. So please, consider what God may be calling you to do in the midst of your surprise. I've seen great outcomes with both; and each have been difficult conclusions to reach.

Remember that one day, this will all pass. In fact, in nine months a decision will have been made and a sweet baby will grace your home or the home of a couple who has longed to lavish a child with love. Since the crisis is going to pass, but you will always have your daughter, love her in such a way that no matter what she does, she will get a sweet taste of the character of God, who promises that nothing she can do can separate her from Him, and hopefully, nothing she can do will separate her from you.

What If My Teen Is a Different Person Online?

"My wife and I recently looked at our daughter's MySpace account. What we found was a little shocking, and even more shocking to see all her friends' spaces. We were floored and angry as we looked at the seductive pictures of herself our daughter posted, and read the unacceptable language (for our home) that she was writing. Is this truly the world that she lives in, and how should we approach our daughter about some things that just aren't true?"

I've never met a young person who hasn't wanted to be cool in the eyes of peers. Wanting to be somebody, wanting to be accepted, and wanting to be loved are normal longings that I've already mentioned. Teens want to catch someone's eye. They hope to be valued among their friends. Acceptance is paramount for teens. Teens want others to know that they have it all together and that they've accomplished something. They want others to sing their praises. They want to be known and revered by others. They want to be liked. They want to be successful. They want a sense of significance.

They want nothing more than what I want.

Yet I have ways to show my success and significance. I can show my success through the possessions that I own, the work that I do, and the house that I have. I can feel significant because of my years of relationships and work. I can display worth and value through the toys that I play with and the places I travel. I can show my success through my family, my grandkids, and my pets. I can show value through my associations, my procreations, my collections, my bank account, and my vocation. I can show a life's purpose fulfilled in a way that I'm happy with, and it can stand for itself. Even my GPS system tells me daily that I have arrived.

How can a teen show the world that they are "worthy" in the eyes of their peers? They did not purchase their own car, and they do not have jobs. They don't have years of relationships, and they don't have kids and grandkids. They don't really have many toys (They play with their family's stuff.) and they can't really travel without Mom and Dad. They haven't collected much, they haven't done much, and the teen years really aren't the best years of their life. They've earned very little, and what they do have has been given to them (generally, in excess).

Most aren't happy with where they are in life and haven't a clue about what their purpose is. But they do have longings for the same things that I long for. And until they learn a little, live a little, and blow out a few more candles, the Internet gives them the opportunity to express those longings. Every teen expresses his or her deep longings in some way. Most teens don't have a house. They don't have a spouse.

But they do have a mouse.

My college degree in finance and real estate investments tells me that "location, location, location" is paramount to value. My minor in marketing tells me that "presentation sells." And my common sense tells me that if I put the two together with a little "networking," I might just get people to pay attention. Whoever has put together the maze of social networking through the Internet has provided a landing place for teens where location and presentation merge with opportunities for networking and interaction. Whether it's MySpace, Bebo, Facebook, Friendster, MyPraize, Hi5, Orkut, YourChristianSpace, or one of the other 300 social networking sites on the Internet, it is a perfect place for the "have-nots" who want desperately to become "haves."

Jason Illian, author of *MySpace, My Kids*, likens teen home pages on MySpace to a house that they can decorate any way they want, where they can show off what they have and display who they are.[1] They can place videos, music, images, comments, thoughts, and wallpaper in any form they want, express whatever they want to whomever they want. They get to invite people to their "home," they have the opportunity to limit who comes to their "home," and they can present themselves as they want to be presented. They can form groups, develop a base of friends, and find things in common with people they don't know.

Do teens exaggerate things about themselves? Is the pope Catholic? Yes, they exaggerate; they are teens. And does this exaggeration cause problems? Sometimes. Should parents be concerned? Perhaps. Should we eliminate the Internet in the lives of our kids because of potential dangers and the not-so-truthful presentations? At times.

I had a young man (one of our teens at Heartlight) at a small group meeting tell me that he has over 4,000 "friends" (other people who agree to be listed) on his MySpace page. He boasted of this number in front of the rest of the group for effect. Was he exaggerating? I looked on his MySpace page and he had 6 "friends." Was I then supposed to go to him and correct him? Not necessarily. But his comments, coupled with what I see in his Internet interaction, give me a clearer picture about who he is and what issues he might be struggling with.

I'm amazed at how some girls present themselves on Internet social networks. I'm equally amazed at how girls talk to one another on the Internet. I would call it "digital courage." Kids get online and say things that they would never say face-to-face. As a result, the presentation online fuels fights in relationships, misinterpretations by guys, and false expectations by those around them. This way of interacting keeps young girls operating on the pettiness level of about seventh grade. That's okay if you're in seventh grade. It's not so okay if you're older.

This past Christmas, I was reading through all the cards that were sent to my wife and me. I love reading Christmas cards. One in particular stood out. It was a picture of a family that looked perfect; everyone looked great, all were smiling, and there were no blemishes in site (amazing what Photoshop will do). The accompanying letter stated how great everyone was doing, how it had been a super year for their family, and how God had blessed them beyond their wildest imagination.

I knew of things in their life that past year that weren't so great and didn't seem so blessed.

The whole truth was that one child in the picture had just completed a long stint in a drug rehab program. One of the other kids had announced to the family earlier in the year that she was a lesbian. And the mother nearly had a nervous breakdown while watching her kids fall apart. So in the Christmas card, was this family exaggerating or distorting? That's not my call, as it truly may have been a blessed year for them. But it goes to show that it's not just kids, teens, and young men and women who are dabbling in a little distorted image projection and "cover-up." *Capiche?*

The bigger issue concerning teens who project false or exaggerated images to others on the Internet is the fact that one day people who know the truth will see that "space," thus creating an integrity issue. The question that parents must be concerned about is whether or not the images their kids are projecting are going to cause some problems or damage relationships. I would encourage parents not to correct everything, understanding that teens exaggerate and want to "look cool," not only online, but also in every aspect of their life. There are some "strike balls" thrown that are better not to take a swing at. Learn to let some things go and not take that swing.

There are, however, some things that need to be corrected, because some images your teens display and can hurt them and comments they make come back to haunt them. Some of their online actions or projections cannot be taken back. Even as I wrote this page, country artist Brad Paisley sang a song called "I'm Cooler Online." In the video that was shown on CMT (Country Music Television), an actress named Maureen McCormick, who played Marcia Brady from *The Brady Bunch* television series a few decades ago, had a starring role. The video is funny, captures the concept of being cooler on the Internet, and is a spoof that will make you laugh. Go to www.YouTube.com and watch it; you will understand what I mean. As I watched the video, I recognized her (We're the same age.) and searched online to find out what she's doing now. The first description that came up was a nude picture of her from thirty years ago.

Kids don't understand this lesson today. They need to know that most times, the Internet is like Las Vegas—What gets on the Internet, stays on the Internet. Pictures on the Internet are like tattoos; you can't always get rid of something you thought was a good idea ten years ago.

Pictures that girls post on the Internet to strut their stuff and be cool will remain on the Internet, if someone captures the picture and reproduces it on other sites. Employers will look at potential employees' pages and use them to judge their character. The display of "partying" pictures has a tendency to move your child into a different category of people. Comments, thoughts, statements, and ramblings are not always good things to share with strangers. Loose lips sink ships.

If you as a parent, youth minister or good friend, feel that what you see online of a young person you know could be potentially damaging, I would suggest that you intervene. A young lady who used to be in our residential program called me and asked if she could come visit with my wife and me and stay for a weekend. I told her that I would get back with her. I got online and looked at her personal Web site and felt a little uncomfortable, as I found sexually aggressive pictures, music depicting sexual acts, a background screen of half-clad women and the word "Playboy" written all over the page. The comments from friends were full of expletives and sexual innuendo. I felt uncomfortable, and even more importantly, I felt like this page was not indicative of the girl I knew, nor was it going to be beneficial for her in her interaction with people. I didn't e-mail her a message letting her know my difficulty with how she was presenting herself; I called her. I made a connection, not just a communication.

My comments to her went something like this:

"Sweetheart, this is not who you are, and it's not what you're about...is it? It's okay to look attractive, but not provocative. It's okay to share some things, but not all things. It's okay to show some things, but not all things. It's okay to say some things, but it's damaging to say others. What do you think?"

She melted a little and heard what I was saying, which never could have been communicated in an e-mail, letter, or voice mail. She just said, "I hear you." I think she heard what I said, and she understood that I was valuing her.

Teens will try to be cool. They have always tried to be cool. They will always try to be cool. And social networking on the Internet will be here from now on. It's not going to change. What can change is the way we approach this medium and format in which our teens express themselves to people. I'll give you some rules and suggestions about the Internet and your teen's use of it later. Right now, it is important for you not to be afraid of all these new opportunities of communication, but to familiarize yourself with the upside and the downside of your child's involvement on the Internet.

Do not trust that your teen will be perfect, that he'll never fall into some areas of concern. Stay engaged with your child and keep a close eye out for any changes in the climate of your teen's attempt to be cooler online.

QUESTION 8

What If Our Teen Is Becoming Someone We Don't Know—Or Like?

"We're seeing stuff from our daughter that we've never seen. It's almost as if she woke up one October day and was a completely different person. We thought we were doing well with our "old" Christie, but we don't have a clue how to handle this new girl living in our home. Help!"

There is nothing worse than living with a teen spinning out of control, and no worse feeling than the hopelessness parents experience in the process. It is difficult to know what to do and how to react when your teen daily reaches new lows in disobedience, dishonesty, and disrespect, when your child seems to delight in choosing every wrong thing.

Your teen is caught in what I call "The Spin Cycle," and he or she needs you to intervene. This downward spiral can have tremendous destructive potential with lifelong consequences. It can even bring a young life to a quick end. When teens spin out of control, they need responsible, loving adults to respond, not react, even if they do everything they can to keep you out of it. In responding to a spiraling teen, you offer calmness, honesty, love, grace and support. If you are reacting to a spiraling teen, you are emotional, angry, hurt, judgmental, and often harsh.

These knee-jerk, seemingly instinctive reactions are almost always counterproductive.

We have all done it. Our teen comes home two hours past curfew. We have been waiting up, worrying about all the possible horrible reasons why he is so late. We're an emotional wreck at this point. Then he calmly waltzes in and ignores us, when we're sitting right there in the chair. That does it! Our brain seems to turn off, and we start yelling, "What have you been doing?" "Where have you been?" "How dare you!" All this does is make him angry, so he yells back. The screaming escalates. He slams back out of the house, jumps into his car and drives away.

Now what?

Reacting to your teen is probably not going to give you the response you wanted. Responding in chaos is difficult and takes lots of practice. Parents of teens must learn to stop their mouths, think about what is being said or done, and then speak or act – Stop, Think, Go.

Most people, especially in times of crisis are in Go, Stop, Think mode, which will only bring more pain and chaos. Now that you have teens, you must learn how to respond to your teen. The avenues of communication this can open will strengthen your relationship. You cannot ignore or overlook inappropriate behavior, but you can't use knee-jerk reactions either.

If your teen is becoming someone you don't know—and don't really like—prepare to act now. Don't wait, and don't ignore the evidence that your teen is spinning out of control. Act today based on what you know is true. You know your faith, your own beliefs, and what you believe is best for your child.

So, Where Do You Start?

You can start with a simple *truth and consequences* message, such as, "Honey, we're not going to live like this anymore" or, "I will no longer stand by and watch you destroy yourself; we're going to address what's going on, get some help, and get through this together." Make the message clear that negative behavior will no longer be allowed or tolerated in your home. Let your child know that if it doesn't stop, he will not be able to live there.

The point is not to kick your teen out so you don't have to worry about her anymore (and you can't just kick her out if she is underage), but you can use the threat of losing the comfort of your home as a tool to get teens thinking about the consequences of continued inappropriate behavior. There are many programs and schools designed to deal with struggling teens and keep them safe, like our Heartlight residential program in Texas. If you need help finding such a program, give me a call and I'll help you find the right one. The fact is, just placing boarding school, boot camp, military school or wilderness therapy program materials on the counter for your teen to see may be enough to get him to sit up and take notice that you are serious about making a change.

Your teen has called your bluff a lot in the past, daring you to enforce your rules. The fact that you have taken the time and effort to research and collect information on several programs can be a real wake-up call. Your teen may decide not to call your bluff and start acting according to your boundaries and rules. If your child doesn't, you have to be willing and able to follow through. If you set a consequence, you must enforce it, no matter how uncomfortable it makes you and your teen. The whole point of consequences is to cause discomfort so that bad behaviors will no longer occur and new, good behaviors will be learned.

Don't expect your teens to like the fact that you are calling a halt to their inappropriate behavior. They probably won't appreciate your attempts to deal with it at all. Their first response will most likely be anger or resentment. Be prepared for their behavior to get worse – more screaming, more name-calling, etc. They are upping the ante, forcing you to stand firm and not back down. They want to see if you are really serious about these new rules. Remember that the time your child may spend hating you is short. Compared to the entirety of a life, it's just a blip on the radar. Secretly, he or she may feel relieved and thankful you cared enough to intervene, giving your teen a good excuse to say "no" to peers when asked to participate in the wrong things.

Usually, teens figure out that life will be much easier if they change their behavior so they can stay at home and work things out with their parents, but not always right away. Sometimes they simply don't figure this out at all.

If They Don't Change, Then What?

Once you start down the path of responsible parenting, don't stop, and don't be pulled down to their level with childish fighting. Stay calm and focused on what you want for them and deal with the heart of the issue. There will be days when you mess up and yell back. After you calm down again, go to your teen and apologize for yelling. Don't turn it into a lecture or blame her for you losing your cool. Owning up to your shortcomings is a powerful way to teach your teen how to become respectful of others and learn conflict resolution. Do not expect your teen to accept your apology. Just put it out there with sincerity and leave it at that. Give her permission to struggle with things, knowing that your love for her will never change. We all struggle.

Teens fear rejection probably more than anything else at this point in their lives. You will need to tell your teen over and over that there is nothing he can do to make you love him less, or anything he can do to make you love him more. This is a message that you will probably need to repeat daily (if not several times a day). It's also a message that you have to believe yourself. It is hard to keep loving someone when he keeps hurting you. But that is exactly your job as a parent.

Up until this point, your teen has probably linked his behavior with your love. Disconnecting the two is vital. Withholding love should never be an option. That is not a valid discipline technique. Withholding parental love increases a teen's hurt, confusion, and anger. All it does is make matters worse! Loving your teen through the bad times is the only way your family will make it through this and come out the other side intact.

Just remember that loving your teen doesn't mean you let him get away with his behavior. The opposite is true. Because you love your teen, you enforce the rules and allow the consequences to be completely felt. Set the limits and boundaries you know he or she needs, and above all be firm. Talk about the new rules and boundaries, so that everyone in the family is clear on the new expectations. Allow your teen input on the consequences. When the rules are broken, enforce the consequences! You have to follow through and be consistent. Otherwise, you just increase the confusion and frustration, provoking your teen to a higher level of rebellion and anger.

Here are some of my top teen Don'ts and Do's:

The Don'ts

Don't act out of anger. Remember Ephesians 4:26 (NIV), "In your anger do not sin."

Don't get physical. If tempers flare and voices are raised, take a break, keep it cool.

Don't ignore what is happening in hopes it will just go away. It won't.

Don't build monuments to your grief, or park yourself in the valley.

Don't give in when you know you should stand your ground.

The Do's

Do put your hope in your faith and act on the Truth.

Do understand that God is teaching both you and your teen during this time.

Do seek help from qualified professionals and connect with support outside your family.

Do handle yourself in a manner that keeps your relationship with your teen alive, as it may determine the kind of relationship you'll have ten years from now.

Do change your own bad habits when it's obviously your fault.

There's never a good time in our busy lives to be faced with a crisis like dealing with a teenager caught in The Spin Cycle. It can be very difficult, but keep in mind that many parents are going through the same thing with their own teenagers. Seek them out and find a place where you can share your feelings and gain strength and support from each other. The struggle may seem endless, and you may feel hopeless at times, but the time to act is *now*, and it may very well save your teen's life. Doing nothing is not an option for a caring parent.

WHEN YOUR TEEN'S CHOICES AFFECT YOU—AND OTHERS

QUESTION 9

What if My Teen Thinks I "Owe" Him Everything?

"My 15-year-old wants everything, all the time, whenever he asks for it. It's almost as if I've been put on this earth as his parent just to give him what he wants. He's demanding, arrogant, unappreciative, and never satisfied, never content. He does nothing but complain about everything I do or say. I'm afraid our family has gotten into a pattern of this, and it's eventually going to drive me nuts. How do I get out of this mess that I've created?"

One of the biggest problems I see with today's teens is an entitlement issue. For a number of reasons, many teens today feel like they're entitled to everything. Want a definition? *Entitlement* means to have title, to own or have a special claim or right to some thing or privilege.[1] The title that you hold on your home, for example, means that you are entitled to all the benefits that come from owning that home. It is yours. You are free to do what you want with it. The problem with teens today is that many lay "title" to that which is not theirs. And if parents aren't careful in their parenting style, they can easily lead a child to believe that he has title to many, many things. Teens, especially, can then develop false expectations about who is going to meet their needs.

As Dr. Tim Kimmel, parenting expert and my friend, recently said on our weekly Heartlight Radio program, "The problem with kids brought up in our typical middle class homes is that they are basically born on third base but are under the delusion they hit a triple."[2] It is from that basis of entitlement that I believe we see young people remaining immature, being neglectful of the assumption of responsibility, treating people disrespectfully, and basically refusing to grow up.

Teens today want more, demand more, and expect more for their lives than any other generation I have known. They indeed feel entitled. And as long as parents are willing to give everything and always meet the needs (and wants) of their teens, they just might be postponing the development of a healthy understanding of life in their teens. Here are some examples:

If a parent always gives their children money, thus eliminating the need for them to work for their funds, then children never learn the value that "A good day's work brings a good day's wages." If a parent always washes a teen's clothes, then a teen never learns to do that so he can function when he leaves home. If a parent is always running to wake up their 17-year-old, that child will not know how to get himself out of bed for school or work when he no longer lives at home. Bottom line: If a parent is meeting all the needs of a teen, why would a teen want anything different?

Let me ask you some other questions. Does your child expect you to buy her a car? Did your parents purchase a car for you when you were that age? Does your child expect you to pay for college? Did you have someone pay for your college? Does your child expect you to pay for car insurance, cell phone, gasoline, dates, clothes, dining out and give an allowance? Is this what you expected? It may not be. But it is what teens today seem to expect—and often are given. Unless a teen is told otherwise, he will continue to receive without giving.

There's nothing inherently wrong with parents wanting to do things for their child. But when a parent's actions keep a child from learning some valuable lessons in life, then a parent might unintentionally not be looking out for the child's best interest. In today's culture, the desire that parents have to provide for their child, coupled with a teen's high expectations and demanding nature, poses a threat to developing maturity and responsibility. Somewhere in the midst of child rearing, many parents forgot to wean their teens from having everything done for them and given to them. This results in a teen's sense of entitlement, which includes assumed expectations. Some teens actually believe that the lifestyle they lived during their pre-teen years, a lifestyle where everything is given and taken care of, should continue well into their teen years. And unless there is a stated and understood change of direction, your teen will carry these expectations and sense of entitlement well beyond their teen years.

My suggestion? State what needs to change and make sure your teen understands. I doubt that many parents can change their teen's culture. But I have no doubt of your ability to change your child's expectations. It's easy—just don't do quite so much. Don't give in to every demand.

I find myself telling teens all the time, "I owe you nothing, but I want to give you everything." What this does is lower the expectation, creates an assumption of their responsibility, and allows me to interact with them on a playing field where I can give them something. It's on this field that perhaps they can begin to understand the definition of the word *grace*...getting something one doesn't deserve.

I find today that so many teens have such high levels of expectation from those in authority over them, that asking for particular privileges and things is predicated on the basis that they are owed or deserved. The asking is not really asking. It then becomes a demand in a pretty form. It's their polite way of demanding that you fulfill the role that they want you to fulfill.

I'm usually pretty straightforward with them. I usually say, *"Thanks for asking. But you want to know something? Every time you ask, I get the feeling that you are really demanding something from me. You spend so much time asking that you give me little or no time to offer or invite you to something other than your demands. I want you to know that I don't owe you anything, but I want to give you everything. You just don't give me the opportunity because you're so busy trying to get what you want."*

It's a mind-set that permeates today's teen culture. They have misinterpreted parents' abundance in giving and think that their parents are just filling their obligations. They demand and don't really think of what they're asking. They lack gratitude when they are given something because they believe (and I have heard them say), *"Why should I be grateful when you should have been doing that anyway?"* They are stuck in a world of entitlement and expectations that is foolish, childish, and immature. And parents get tired of it quickly. Because as a teen ages, the prices of toys increase, the demands are greater, and their lack of assuming responsibility for their lives becomes more obvious and detrimental.

Entitlement doesn't serve anyone well—not the child who doesn't grow up or the parents who feel used. Want a good biblical basis for my comments? Take a look at the story of the Prodigal Son in the fifteenth chapter of Luke. Allow me to pull out four verses from that story to make my point. It's a wonderful story of grace, a story where a father, a son, an older son, and others give us insight into a world of entitlement and how a father allowed that mind-set to be broken.

In Luke 15:12 a younger son says to his dad, "'Father, give me my share of the estate.'" For whatever reason, this son has a sense of entitlement that is pretty strong and demanding. *"Give me what you owe me."* Sound Familiar? Well, this father gave it to him. Maybe the dad had an ulterior motive. Maybe he was just worn out and gave in. I know some families who would give away everything they owned just to get some relief from having to deal with a demanding son.

Anyway, the son took what was given to him and spent it. What a great lesson in finance! His life deteriorated until he had nothing, and he tried to eat pigs' slop. Now that's a young man in want. The people around him, who were either sick of his begging or very wise, responded like this: "but no one gave him anything" (Luke 15:16). They gave him nothing. They quit giving. They demanded, by their actions, something different for the life of this young man. They didn't bail him out or allow him to continue in his foolishness, and here's what happened next: "...he came to his senses." (Luke 15:17).

The prodigal son saw the light. Because he could no longer look to the people who gave him everything, he was moved to look somewhere different. And when he looked somewhere different, he saw something different. That difference wasn't about the fact that his father didn't give him enough money, or that the people around him didn't help him enough. In fact, everyone quit doing what they could do and allowed this young man to face some pretty important issues in his life. Then "*he came to his senses.*" His father didn't change him. His family didn't change him. The younger son learned his lesson. When the son's heart was moved and his eyes were opened, his life changed. He went home a new man, humble and willing to accept the most menial position—to earn his way—if his family would have him. His father welcomed him home.

When the older brother responded to the prodigal's return with disdain and even jealousy at the fact that their father greeted him so warmly after he had wasted everything he was given, the older son received an important lesson about grace.

"'My son,' the father said. 'You are always with me, and everything I have is yours.'" (Luke 15:31). Both sons receive grace—one after his demands and sense of entitlement, one for his arrogance and envy. Both examples are beautiful.

Here's my bridge. Until someone quits giving, teens will not come to their senses and begin to understand life, relationships, and grace. Giving something when it is demanded is not grace. Grace is getting something you don't deserve. And in a world where teens feel like they deserve everything, the message of grace, God's free gift, is lost. It's lost because, in our attempt to give our kids everything, we've destroyed our child's ability to understand what grace is. We haven't helped; we've hindered. And we've got stop giving in and help our child understand healthy adult relationships—and a healthy relationship with God.

Parents who feel like they are giving grace to their teen by giving everything or who do not require mature and responsible behavior are not giving grace at all. They are enabling. And it is that kind of enabling that will ruin your child. Maybe you are the one keeping your child from growing up. Is it possible that you might be contributing to your teens' "prodigal" status by catering to them and not demanding that they grow up? It might be painful to take a good, hard look at yourself, but that pain is nothing compared to living for decades with a "grown" child who continues to depend on you and never grows up.

Let your kids know that you owe them nothing, but want to give them everything. It's a lesson they'll thank you for one day.

And it's a lesson that puts you in a position to teach them about grace and giving. It's time, Mom and Dad, to help your child come to his senses and quit being that prodigal. The answer might not be for him to leave, but it may very well be that he quit acting like a demanding, entitled, selfish prodigal. Teens may need to get a job, set an alarm clock, learn which knobs are which on the washing machine, and get paid only for what they earn around the house. Hard work won't hurt them; it may very well save them.

What If My Kid's Behavior Is Driving Me Nuts?

"Our son was adopted 15 years ago, and it has been a struggle to raise him. He has ADHD and has trouble focusing, doesn't respect authority, doesn't care what we think or want, and doesn't care about anyone other than himself. He will still do chores and schoolwork, but only after I have nagged him to death (and nagging drives me nuts!). He's angry all the time. He has physically challenged me. He blames others for things that happen in his life and spends his days wasting time and achieving nothing. Living with our son has caused our family incredible stress. We have no more ideas for how to help him. Do you?"

If you're in a situation even somewhat similar to this one, you've got your hands full. Adopted. Attention Deficit Disorder with Hyperactivity. Lack of respect for authority. Extreme selfishness. Anger. Physically challenging. Blames others. Low achiever. I would imagine that you have incredible family stress! When it rains, it pours. From experience, I would also speculate that all the struggles with one child in the family cause struggles in your marriage, siblings, and the operation of the home, thus increasing stress that shows itself in other areas.

The tendency is to lump everything together into one huge and overwhelming mess, which compounds feelings that there will never be any resolution. Let me assure you that your situation can change. More importantly, there is hope. Not only *can* you get to the other side of the struggles you're now facing, you *will* get to the other side. I would encourage you to not let the enormity of what you see make your hope of a solution small.

One thing that can't change is the fact that in this case, the son was adopted. All the other challenges have the possibility of change. Every situation that I face with parents is unique in its makeup, thus unique in its resolution. No two answers will be the same for any family. But there are some similarities that can give you some direction.

Fifteen is the age when a young man starts exercising his manhood, while still wanting to hold on to his boyish and childhood ways. It's a time where two oceans of different thoughts and expectations collide as the waves of change come rolling in. It's the end of an era and the beginning of another. It's a time of increased hormones, a move from concrete to abstract thinking, and the point when growth spurts make a young man feel both bold and awkward.

Because it's a time of such great transition for your teen, there must also be a change in the way you operate your home. It's time to stop operating under the ways that worked for your child (and that are no long effective), and start with some new directions and expectations that fit your young man. Your son treats you the way he does because he can. Your current system of operation has allowed him to treat you as he pleases. For him to operate differently, the system of operation has to change.

I always encourage parents to develop a Belief System for Discipline in their home. It's a simple plan that is based upon the assessment of areas that need to change within your family, paired with newly established rules and consequences that will be enacted based on the path your teen chooses to take. Teens will continue their inappropriate behavior until the pain they receive as a consequence from that particular behavior is greater than the pleasure they get from their actions.

Here are some thoughts to consider while developing the core Belief System for your home. The intent is to create an atmosphere that allows relationships to flourish and gives your son some control over his choices, which will hopefully help him develop responsibility and maturity, two necessary components of adulthood.

Adoption

In the description of this son, there is one thing that is unchangeable - the fact that he was adopted. In your family, maybe your teen also has a factor that is unchangeable. He lives between two homes. He uses a wheelchair. Whatever the issue, perhaps God wanted him in your family, knowing that he would encounter problems and would need parents like you to help him through these difficult times. Remember that the fingerprint of God you saw on his life at the beginning doesn't disappear because of inappropriate behavior or careless and selfish thinking.

Adopted kids, in particular, wrestle with deep identity issues. They want to know why they were abandoned by their mothers. The concrete thinking of childhood allows a child to understand the concept of adoption through the simple realization of, *"I have a mother somewhere else, and have a mommy that I live with now."* It's pretty simple. As kids move into adolescence and abstract thinking, they begin to emotionally explore the harder issues of value, rejection, and abandonment. The lingering question, *"Why would my mother do that?"* plays in their minds.

If you have an adopted teen who is struggling through the normal issues of a 15-year-old, the adoption issue will be about value, and why the one who should have valued him the most gave him up. It will be important that you affirm his value to you, thus trying to counteract the loss of value that he might feel during his emerging new feelings. Let him know that there is nothing he can do to make you love him more, and nothing he can do to make you love him less, constantly affirming his place with you through words, pictures around the house, and introductions to friends that don't include the word "adopted."

In time, he'll understand all his feelings surrounding his adoption. I've seen that this enlightenment usually doesn't happen until teens age into their mid-twenties. I don't know the reason why it is this way...it's just what I've observed enough to believe that it's true.

Until he gets to that point, he may "act out" his feelings of rejection by his birthmother to justify his unresolved questions of who he is. Furthermore, he may look at you, his adoptive mother or father, and be reminded of what was lost at the beginning of his life. It's a perception thing and a recurring "thinking loop" that will continue until he moves to resolution. I would define a "thinking loop" as a constant mulling over or a continuous train of thought that never resolves but keeps playing over and over in a teen's mind. These loops may be frustrating at best, and depressing at worst. Many times, these loops are put to rest after there is exposure to others who have experienced the same thing, or resolution may come through meeting with a counselor that is acquainted with this struggle and can walk with your teen through this time of questioning.

Attention Deficit Disorder (ADD) with Hyperactivity (ADHD)

If your son has a short attention span, then try shortening the way that you communicate or the way that you expect him to learn. Long lectures won't work, and lengthy conversations won't stick. The key to helping many ADD teens learn is through a series of shorter messages, rather than depending on one longer message.

Another thing to note about ADD teens is that they often have an easier time forgiving and forgetting, because they don't dwell on things too long. They'll be the ones who are ready to move on to the next thing and will not feel remorse as long as others, either. The short attention span, not just applicable to academic situations, affects the watching of TV programs, deep discussions about spiritual topics or the morning news, completing tasks and chores, and focusing long enough on a particular topic to go deeper rather than just staying in the shallow end. Many would prefer a *USA Today* newspaper over reading a lengthy novel. They would rather "do" than just "be," and enjoy activity over rest. It's the nature of the way they're wired.

On the positive side, ADD folks can multi-task, doing a number of things at the same time. They can listen to music on a headset, watch TV, do homework, and eat dessert all at the same time. They make great salesmen, are great communicators, and possess a good sense of quick-witted humor. They make great debaters and wonderful lawyers. The hyperactivity side of ADHD means that they'll need to burn off energy in a way that is different from playing video games or surfing the Internet. They need physical activity to burn off energy and multi-sensory stimulation.

I know this person well. I am he.

Lack of Respect

This is a key issue. I would let a teen know, without question, that there will be respect given to each person in the home. Of course, this means that parents can't be disrespectful to their teens too. Once parents identify the need for mutual respect within the home, use a family dinner as the setting to communicate your new commitment that each person should respect the others in the family. Tell your family that you would like to have a family dinner to discuss some things. Don't tell them what you're going to talk about. Deep family communication can be lost in the premature passing of information from parents who can't wait for the most effective time to share news. In other words, wait until the meal to share what you want to communicate.

Give your family some time to wonder about what's going to be said so that they come to the table with a sense of curiosity, not already "bored out of their gourd" thinking that they're going to have to sit through *another one of Mom's or Dad's rants.* Prepare or purchase the favorite meal of the person that you're having the most problems with. (Don't tell him that you did this, and don't tell him why you did it.) When you sit down, start the conversation by admitting that you have been disrespectful to members of your family. You will set the tone for the meal, and give an example of what you would like to see. The conversation starter might sound like this:

> *"I want you guys to know that I have failed you as a family in the area of respect. I believe that each person around this table deserves my respect. I have not always given it, and I have not protected all of you from disrespect. Both areas are going to change, and it's going to start with me. So I want to say I'm sorry for all the times that I have not been sensitive to you, your music and TV shows,*

*your needs, your wants, or maybe just your time. I want
things around here to be different. What do you guys (or
girls) think?"*

Let them talk. Don't explain away anything. Don't give excuses.
Just let them talk, and you listen. If there is a point that needs to
be addressed, address it later, or just say, *"Matt, I'd like to discuss
that further later...I'm a little uneasy with that."* You don't have to
resolve everything in one setting.

Here's the kicker. At the end of the discussion, you say
something like this that puts the bite into your message: *"Thanks
for talking. And if you didn't talk, thank you for listening. Because
I want people to be respected within our family, I think that we're
going to implement some new rules about the presence of disrespect
in our home. We just can't allow its presence to hurt the relationships
in our home, or disrupt the way that we function."*

This is when you tell them that you want to get together the
following week and lay out some ideas about disrespect and the
consequences for its presence. Those consequences might include
taking away the car keys, cell phone, car insurance, allowance,
computer, video game stations, Internet privileges, or participation
in something that is dearly liked. Place the greatest consequences
where your greatest desire is for change in your family. There's no
doubt in my mind that the issue of respect is a key issue.

Your Teen's Selfishness

Parents feed their teen's selfishness by continuing to rotate life
around the teen beyond the beginning of their adolescent years, at
which time parents should be aggressively jumpstarting them out
of their selfish mind-set of always being served into learning how
to serve. The command in Scripture, *"Do not think of yourself more
highly than you ought..."* (Romans 12:3, NIV), is a good principle
to teach your teens, as selfishness that is allowed to grow during
the teen years will only accentuate other problems and bring more
problems to the forefront as they get older.

How do you stop your teen's childish selfishness?

First, as stated before, you need to stop doing everything for
your teen. Quit jumping every time he says "frog." Review the
negative patterns you established in your home in the early years,

and let it be known in a gentle way that you're no longer going to do some things that you've been doing. Here are some examples:

- I'm no longer going to be doing your laundry.
- I'm no longer going to get you out of bed in the morning.
- I'm no longer going to accept your whining about everything.
- I'm no longer going to be able to be able to throw your paper route for you, do your chores, or type your homework.
- I'm no longer going to nag you about what you need to accomplish.
- I'm no longer going to pay for gas for your car.
- I'm no longer going to clean your room, your bathroom, or make your bed.

Get my point? You have to stop doing some things, so that your child can start doing some things. You stop; your teen starts. Every responsibility that you assume for him is one less responsibility he has to assume. He remains his immature self, because he's not being required to grow up. He's being allowed, and even enabled, to continue in his childish antics. So the first step is to stop.

Second, there needs to be a discussion about why you're going to stop. I would leave the answer as a simple, "Because I don't want to do it anymore." Any comments beyond that will only stir up further fruitless discussion. Let him know that you're not doing it (whatever *it* is) because you don't want to do it anymore. You'll be amazed how this will put your teen in a position of not being so demanding of you, and will put you in a position of not having to do everything.

Give your teen a timeframe, so that he will have to start these new responsibilities this summer or when school starts or when he turns 16 or yesterday or the first of the year. Prepare him that change is coming, and then let him know the following:

- *You're going to have to start doing your laundry.*
- *I've bought you an alarm clock so you can wake yourself up and get yourself to school on time. It's your responsibility.*
- *You can talk to me, but you can't be whiny or disrespectful.*
- *I'll help with your paper route only on bitterly cold days, will do your chores only if you're sick, and type your homework if your fingers are broken (use a little humor).*

- *You'll have to find a girlfriend to nag you, because I'm not doing it anymore. I'll ask once and that's it.*
- *You're going to have to earn some money to pay for your own gas for the car. I'll pay for the insurance; you pay for the gas.*
- *You're going to have to clean your own room. If you want to live in a dump, that's your choice. If you want a clean bathroom, I'll purchase the cleaning materials. Change your own light bulbs, wash your own towels, and scrub your own toilet. I can't do those things because I can't breathe when I'm in your room for the smell of the dirty shoes, socks and shorts.*

I'm sure that when you present these things to your child, you'll get to see his selfishness in action. Let him know that you're more than willing to talk, but not to be disrespected. (Remember the new consequences for disrespect?) If he disrespects you, he'll still have the chores, and a consequence too. The pressure mounts, and that's a good thing.

Doing Chores and Homework

He does these, so reward these. Let him know that if he completes the semester with all his homework turned in (or certain grades achieved) you'll give him one hundred dollars. If you're sitting there with your jaw dropped, thinking, "Mark, do you realize how much that is?" Absolutely! You're going to give it to him in some form at some time anyway, so you might as well give it when he's being affirmed for something positive, at a time when this small donation might save you from having to make a greater donation later.

Pay him for chores around the house with the condition that you're not going to remind him of when those chores need to be completed. No IOU's or prepayments. He gets the cash when he completes the task. And if he does a good job, throw in a tip to let him know your appreciation. It's amazing how small, affirming actions promote better behavior, because if you're having to deal with all these other issues, you're going to need some bright spots where he feels affirmed and connected to you in some way.

Anger

Anger is an emotional response to not getting what you want. When your son gets angry, what is he not getting that he wants? Does he know? Does he get angry because he is being provoked? Is there an excessive amount of stress in his life? Could he be angry because he is realizing that he is a selfish, disrespectful, hyperactive, angry, low achiever? If that's the case, then the display of anger could be the first step in the right direction to make some changes.

Anger's not always a bad thing. Being disrespectful and physically aggressive are wrong, but anger shows that people want something, and the intuitive parent will look beyond the symptom (anger) to what is really going on in the child's heart (What is your teen longing for?). Once you find out what he wants, then express your desire to help him have that need met. Don't rescue him from his anger, but help him find the source of it.

If his type of anger is one that won't release and is a constant—where he gets up angry, goes to bed angry, and let's everyone know he is angry in between—I would strongly encourage you to require counseling. Angry teens are going to release their anger somewhere, so get help for them in managing it if they are consumed or overwhelmed with its hold on their lives.

Physically Challenging

This is an easy one for me. The message I give to parents and to teens without hesitation is, "If you ever get physical with me, I will have you arrested." No excuses. No exceptions. No misunderstandings. You touch me, and you'll end up in the back of a police car going somewhere.

If you have a teen that is so out of control that he (or she) would become physical with anyone in the family, then you do need outside help. I wouldn't hesitate to get that help from police, even if you are embarrassed to see them pulling up to your home. If their involvement protects you and others in your family, then I would request the police send ten cars with lights on and sirens blasting.

If your son spends one night in juvenile detention, that is far better than spending a lifetime in prison. If he spends one night locked up, it is better than being locked out of your home. The message has got to be, "Do not get physical." Period.

Blames Everyone Else

This is more of a sign of irresponsibility than anything else. It's a childish habit that is being carried over to adolescence. It should stop when you begin to initiate all these other recommendations that I'm suggesting. But there is another point to be touched on here. There are times when I ask teens a question about their lying and their blaming of everyone else for their actions. The question is, "Why is it so hard for you to be wrong?"

Some teens feel like it's a sign of weakness at a time in their life when they want to appear strong. Some have been told that they can't be wrong. Some have been taught that they need to be perfect, so they won't admit being wrong, as it would destroy their goal. Some feel that if they are wrong, they will lose the relationship with their parents, so they lie and blame others for their wrongdoing. Some are scared to be wrong because they secretly believe that might be why they were given up for adoption—because they weren't good enough. Some will deflect any responsibility, because to be wrong would mean that everyone else is right and justified. Some have been told, through the abusive actions of others, that they are trash. So to be wrong (and look like trash, in their eyes) is not an option. So they blame others. And they lie about their actions. Under these circumstances, wouldn't you?

I find that in the above types of situations, it's often the parent who is responsible for creating the environment in which a teen feels he can't afford to be wrong. If the parents instilled the belief, even inadvertently, it may take a counselor to walk this path with your child, or a concerned youth worker, youth minister or family friend to ask some hard questions.

Here's a real tough reason why some kids blame others. I think this condition might be genetic. I see lots of parents who are scared to death to admit they are wrong. This might have been passed down. You think?

Low Achiever

If your teen is a low achiever, then offer some incentives to help him get motivated to put out the extra effort that will be needed to get where he needs to be. Offer rewards for accomplishments and accolades for goals met. It's a simple concept too readily ignored, as some parents think that they're bribing their kids to do well. I agree with that concept. I wouldn't consider it bribery; I would consider it manipulation. (I laugh as I write that, so you should laugh as you're reading it.) Chances are you know what your child wants and what he would like to possess. You also know where his lack of motivation is and are quite familiar with his areas of underachievement. If there is a way to connect those two together, I encourage parents to do so. Instead of spending so much money on birthdays and Christmas, spread the funds throughout the year to keep your teen tracking year 'round.

There's a difference between being performance-based and performance-oriented. Performance-based relationships give or take away love or value based on what a child does or doesn't do. This is not a good foundation for relationship, as it becomes somewhat conditional on the accomplishments of a teen. But there's nothing wrong with being performance-oriented, which is a desire to have your teen accomplish as much as possible, to fully become the person God created your child to be.

If your teen is a low achiever because of a learning disability or difficulty, then expectations need to be adjusted accordingly. I'm not sure that more time needs to be spent on testing, but on highlighting something your child enjoys doing. In other words, trying again and again and again to get a frog to fly, testing him to see what he needs to be able to fly, and forcing him to practice flying when it's just not what he was created to do frustrates everybody. A frog is never going to be a good flyer, But a frog is an excellent hopper. So instead of trying to turn your "frog" into a mediocre flyer, at best, work on his hopping! Help him be the best hopper he can be, and you know what? You'll reduce stress and increase your enjoyment of each other.

I know plenty of parents who have reduced their level of stress, for example, by reducing the standards by which they measure their child's academic progress. I'm a living example of one who made "C's" all through junior and senior high, didn't rank in the top sixty percent of my class, and wasn't motivated to get any higher grades. I was excited about activities, social environments, athletics, and anything that didn't cause me to have to think too much. And guess what? Those are the abilities that help me connect with teens today. I still have to use my brain to write, but I can always hire an editor to be my "smarts."

This has been a long chapter. It's long because it deals with many issues and behaviors that need to be changed or brought into line with what parents want for their teen. If these behavior patterns are allowed to continue, the young man in this question—and your teen, if these behaviors apply to your child—will learn the harder lessons through more severe consequences at a later age, when a husband or wife and kids might be possibly be involved.

Not to discourage you in any way, but perhaps the length of the chapter is indicative of the length of time it will take to get through these issues too. Your teen just didn't get here overnight, so chances are good that he's not going to get away from these habits and behavior patterns overnight. It will take time, perhaps a long time. But however long it takes, the results will be better if you have a strategy than if you don't do anything at all.

QUESTION 11

What If We Don't Have a Clue What's Going on?

"We're lost and haven't a clue what is happening in the life of our young daughter. She's depressed, doesn't want to go to school, is sad, and doesn't talk much anymore. Our relationship is still good, but most of our inquiries as to, "What's going on?" are answered with the usual "I don't know." Please don't tell us you don't know, either."

I may not have all the answers, but I can tell you that there's a good chance your daughter really doesn't know what's happening within herself. It sure sounds like you have a depressed young lady in the house. She has shut down, and you're going to need to approach this differently than you have been. If she doesn't know what she is feeling, she's hardly going to be able to describe it when you ask, *"What's going on?"* She may not know the words to describe new feelings that she's having. But just because a teen can't describe something, doesn't mean she doesn't feel it.

In this case, ask her to go on a walk with you and make it a regular weekly (or daily) event. I call these simple times "walk and talks." If she refuses, just let her know that you think that it's important for you and her to spend some time together. I would suggest that you have this type of conversation with her:

"Sweetheart, I know that something's not right. And we love you too much to just sit back and do nothing. You're losing credit in school, you're becoming distant,

*and you're falling into a funk that's just not a good place
to be. We're going to have to find some answers, because
you evidently don't know what's going on, and neither
do we. I'm just trying to see if we can find some common
ground where we can come up with some answers. I'd like
for us to walk together, go get a cup of coffee, something
to eat, or just hang out. But we've got to get up and do
something. I can't just sit and do nothing."*

You've made your case. You've asked. And you've let her know
that you're not going to do nothing. Her response will let you know
where to go in your strategy of finding out what's happening inside
her head and heart.

I've found that the strong-arm tactics and the get-your-rear-
out-of-bed-and-get-to-school-or-else drill sergeant approach just
don't work like they did twenty years ago. Teens just don't respond
in a positive way to those anymore. If they do respond, chances are
they'll get out of bed, go to school, and just transfer the problem
to another location. Encourage, invite, and warmly approach your
teen who is depressed. You don't want to push your teen over the
edge when she is depressed by venting your frustration when both
you and she don't know what's going on in her life.

If she says "okay," then go out and walk. Ask a few questions.
Don't play "Twenty Questions" or badger her. The intent is to let
her know that you are a safe, welcoming place to talk.

If she says "no," then tell her that you want her to think about it
and you'll talk later that day, after dinner, or tomorrow. If she is still
negative to the thought of spending time talking, then I'd tell her
that you feel it is important enough to talk that if she is unwilling,
you're going to treat her refusal as an act of disobedience and take
something away that she won't get back until she walks and talks.

Parents always ask, "What do you take away?" I offer the same
suggestions I have before, you take away what hurts—and what
hurts a teen most? Take away the cell phone, computer, car, gas
money, TV, an iPod or anything that she loves and will miss. She
may respond and say, "Fine, go ahead and take it away. I don't
care." Then leave it alone and let the absence of the item have its
effect. She may come to you later and say, "Okay, let's talk," and
may only be doing it to get her missing item back. But so what if

her motives aren't pure? You now have an opportunity to try to reach her heart.

If she is overly adamant about not talking, then she needs to know that she'll have to talk with someone else if not you. A youth pastor, a friend, a counselor, someone she's close to, or someone who can speak to her heart. The message over and over to her that she needs to hear is that you are not going to sit and do nothing. She can be a part of the process or be absent from it, but your intent is to help her through whatever it is that she's dealing with. You're not going to stop.

Your course of action, should she be persistent in not talking to anyone, should be an age-appropriate and calculated strategy as to how to approach the next step in finding out the real problem at hand. This is the time for you to ask questions of other people, seek counsel, read articles, and search for answers. A teen that is so depressed that she is shutting down, not talking, and not wanting to go to school is not normal. So you can't just sit back and wait for these symptoms of depression to pass. The situation should be taken seriously and a course of action planned.

I'm not a medical doctor and can't give any medical advice, but I will tell you that before you'll make progress with a child who has shut down, you will have to deal with the depression. Until she is out from under the cloud of "gloom and doom" that is hanging over her, the responses you hear and the actions you see will come from that depression. Call your doctor and ask for help.

Once your child is willing to talk, or willing to walk, ask questions. These might be:

- What scares you the most about going to school?
- Is going to school harder than you thought it was going to be?
- Which is harder at school, the social part or the academic part?
- Tell me about a time when someone has said something that hurt you.
- Has anyone ever tried to do anything inappropriate with you?
- How are you getting along with the boys?

- What new things have you learned about yourself in school this year?
- How are you doing in your classes?
- What's been the most embarrassing thing that's happened to you in the last month?

Don't share your opinions about her thoughts the first time that you are together. Merely gather information. If she asks you a question, instead of answering it, you might want to say, "I'd like to think about that for a day and I'll get back with you on it." Then plan to get together the next day. What you are doing is creating an environment for dialogue, an arena of relationship, and an atmosphere of trust. You don't have to fix everything today. Your purpose in getting together the first time is to hear her out and to establish a safe foundation. "Be quick to listen, slow to speak and slow to become angry" (James 1:19, NIV). Know that it's okay to have some silent steps on your walk. You may walk around an entire block and not say a word.

I know that this is hard for some of you moms, but you must try to create a environment where your child knows she can talk. If you are talking all the time, she'll clam up and shut down. This isn't your time...it is hers. So let her have the chance to share what's on her heart.

Where you go from that point, I honestly can't tell you. This discussion could lead in a million different directions depending on her comments, observations, and reflections. Once you know what you're dealing with, you'll be better able to plot your course to navigate through your daughter's abnormal behavior.

Here are some of the things I've see other teens struggle with that led to a shutdown or depression:

- Poor choices that led to them feeling stupid or shamed by their peers.
- Ridiculing and hurtful comments from others about their dress, weight, hair, or accent (or anything else that makes them different).
- Traumatic experiences from childhood that are just surfacing now (divorce, sexual abuse, death, adoption).
- Shame over the poor choices they've made (drinking the first time, an experimental sexual experience, taking

inappropriate pictures or videos and sending those to friends, saying the wrong thing at the wrong time.)

- Rejection by former friends, an athletic team, or social clubs.
- Disappointment with friends, their loyalty or their choices.
- Not performing well enough in various arenas where they had high expectations.

Whatever the reason for a shutdown, I encourage parents to become involved before it leads to a meltdown. I've always found that, for teens I walk and talk with, my presence and concern are far more appreciated than the words or wisdom shared. Might I encourage you to do the same? You will then find out some answers to the question of, "What's going on?"

Should I Tell My Teen About My Past?

*"As parents, do we or do we not tell our kids about
any drug experimentation or sexual history in our
past? If we do, when and how much do we tell? I
don't want my child to say, 'Well, Mom and Dad
did it and they're doing okay, so why can't I?' More
importantly, I don't want my children to put me on
a pedestal and think I can't relate, that I don't know
what they're going through or what kind of decisions
they're having to make. I want my kids to be able
to come to me and talk about it. I know they might
not tell me everything, but I want them to know they
can, especially when it comes to really important,
potentially life-changing decisions."*

My wife and I have had golden retriever dogs since we were first married. We currently have four, ages three to eighteen. Their personality and temperament have always held me somewhat captive, as they always greet me with a wag of the tail and an attitude that makes me feel I can do no wrong. A few years ago one of our staff gave me a T-shirt that said, *"Be the kind of person your dogs think you are."* Laughing as I read the slogan, it caused me to understand why dogs are man's best friend. They see us as perfect. And that's how it will stay… because they're dogs.

My wife and I have two granddaughters, ages two and seven. Their personalities and temperament have held me captive, as they always greet me with a "Hi, Poppa," a hug, and an attitude that makes me feel like I can do no wrong. A few years ago, my granddaughter gave me a T-shirt that said, "I love my Poppa." Laughing as I read the slogan, it caused me to understand why grandchildren are so special. They see us as never doing anything wrong. Unlike my dogs, however, that is a place they will *not* stay, as they will one day turn into teenagers.

Any parent would be naïve to think that the ideal and perfect view of their parents that a child possesses in early years would remain throughout their transition into the teen years. As children reach their adolescent years, that perfect world image that some emerging teens possess begins to deteriorate as they experience the hardship of those middle school grade years. They begin to change emotionally. They transition from concrete thinking to abstract thinking. Their bodies begin to change. Their social needs and experiences change. And somewhere along this path, innocence begins to slip away with exposure to new things, new thinking, and new experiences.

They no longer think they are perfect. Their perfect world gets lost. Not everyone gets a trophy for participation. Not everyone wins. Hormones, acne, puberty, social awkwardness, rejection, and new competition greet the new middle schoolers. It's a tough time to say the least. Is it any wonder that most people come to Christ at this time of their life? The need is never more real, and the cry for help is never more needed. Unfortunately, it is also the beginning of a time when parents often become less involved in the life of their child.

All that being said, my answer to the above question about parents sharing their history is a resilient "yes." This is the point when a child needs more than anything to hear that he is not the only one in the world who is struggling. I believe that this is the most important of times for adolescents—when they struggle to find answers spiritually, emotionally, physically and intellectually. It is difficult, challenging, and painful for your teen. No wonder it can also be difficult, challenging, and painful for you. A vast majority of the two thousand young people who have lived with us at our residential program started to get into trouble because of decisions they made during their early teen years.

A parent must be prudent about what is shared. What may be okay to share with a seventeen-year-old daughter about a mom's teenage sexual experience is not okay to share with a twelve-year-old son. Drug usage is not to be bragged about in any way, even if a dad is trying to convince his new teen son or daughter that he used to be cool once. Sinful experiences should only be shared as a point of understanding; an I've-been-there attempt to connect in a new way. Sharing your history of past mistakes and experimentations should be part of a discussion, not the focus of any discussion.

Many people ask why I feel that we should share our faults, mistakes, failures, regrets, and unwise choices with our teens. I feel strongly that we have got to help our teens realize that their perceived parent perfection of days gone by was just that, a perception. Sharing our fallibility won't shatter their concept of who parents are, nor will this enlightenment destroy a relationship with a teen. It will probably affirm what they already know, and let them feel a little more comfortable in their imperfect skin, knowing that they are surrounded by family that truly understands their current condition.

Today's teens aren't impressed that I can play the guitar. They really don't seem to care that I write books, speak around the country, know some pretty famous people, and have a big mustache. They don't give a rip about the fact that I'm on about three thousand radio stations a day, or that I was a pretty successful athlete. It doesn't matter to them that I am a father, husband, uncle, grandfather, son, or brother. They're not impressed by my photography, and they don't bat an eyebrow at the fact that I've been married thirty-three years.

The connection that I get with teens is when I tell them that my wife and I have been in counseling for one-and-a-half years. They connect when they hear me say that I cuss a lot in my head. They connect when they find out that I've heard the words, "Your tumor has spread." They feel something with me when I share my struggles, my hurts, and my misguided stupid mistakes. They relate when I share feelings of depression and discouragement. Oddly, they connect with me when I share what angers me, where I have been missed, and where I have missed the hearts of my children and my wife.

That's funny to me. It's funny that all I've worked for doesn't really measure up to much when it comes to ministry with people.

What does matter is all the mess I've caused, been in, seen, or tasted. So I share more of the mess than the accomplishments, and I get an even greater connection. Do you want to know why people connect at this level? Because that is where they are, and then they feel comfortable sharing their struggles. Want to get someone to talk about their hurts? Talk about yours.

By taking advantage of the sharing opportunities before you with your teens, you are helping them realize that you are not all you're cracked up to be.

You're a lot more.

You're a lot more than what they have seen because you share more of who you are, more of your story, and more about the need in your life for a Savior who promises to take all those imperfections and use them for His cause, His purpose, and His people.

The message that your teens hear is that you just might be normal, and that's a good place to be in the life of your teen. The fear that your child might take what you say and justify his own inappropriate behavior is a justified concern. So take charge of that fear and let him know that it is because of what you have done that you are so adamant about making sure that he doesn't follow the same path.

A man came up to me at a recent seminar that I led and shared with me how he was raised in a perfect family in a perfect town, with a perfect Dad who never did anything wrong. He said that his Dad served on the church deacon board, was president of the local high school booster club, was given awards for all his wonderful service, and was recognized by the governor of his state for being an outstanding citizen. This man stated that he grew up seeing perfection, eating dinner with it every night, and watching perfection play out in his family.

They were perfect—until the day his perfect dad left their perfect home and ran off with the secretary from his perfect company. I said to the man, "Wow, it must have been devastating for you!"

I'll never forget his answer.

"No, it gave me hope," he said.

How Do We Let Go of Our Old Ways?

"Our daughter used to love playing the piano and soccer. She used to love going shopping with me. Now she hates going on vacations, doesn't watch movies with us, and doesn't like our church. We used to have so much fun with her, and she's changed. How do we connect with her again?"

Have you ever had a child balk at your ideas or run from your suggestions, even when you knew life could be better if she followed your advice? Do you have a teen that would rather do it "his way" than your way? Did he used to willingly do what you thought was best, but not anymore? Did he used to enjoy the same things you do? What's happening now? All of a sudden (or so it seems), your teens no longer do what they used to do, or act as they used to. Let me assure that this is part of the natural process of growing up.

While your teen was a child, she believed that you knew everything, and she wanted to please you. As a teen, her motivations are now to think for herself (and prove that you don't know everything) and discover what makes her happy. Sometimes that means doing a 180-degree turn from where she was just days ago.

Let me offer some advice from a lesson I learned when our Heartlight Residential Counseling Center received the gift of two Tennessee Walkers (horses). They are wonderfully spirited horses that we named Knox and Nash, in honor of their Tennessee roots.

The easy part was accepting the gift. The hard part was loading the two powerful animals into an unfamiliar trailer and keeping them calm enough to move them just a few miles to their new home at Heartlight.

The first horse, Nash, loaded up easily. She was older and trusted me to walk her in without a fuss. We hoped Knox would load up just as readily, but as his handler approached the ramp with Knox in tow, he yanked on the horse's lead as if to remind Knox who was "boss." In the process, he also closed Nash's side of the trailer, so Knox couldn't see his lifelong buddy already inside. What's worse, the handler allowed his dog to nip at the horse's heels to try and get him moving onto the loading ramp. Everyone there soon learned that you can't manhandle a horse into a trailer, especially not Knox.

The handler yanked, pulled, tugged, jerked, and wrenched on the rope for quite some time, but Knox stubbornly refused and responded by planting his feet and jerking backwards. The harder Knox was tugged, the more he resisted.

I watched with gritted teeth as a second person decided to "help" by picking up and pulling one of the horse's legs in order to coax him onto the ramp. Knox, who was by now pretty furious about being yanked around by the head, nipped at by a dog, and grabbed at—lost it. He went berserk!

Knox lunged straight up in the air, narrowly missing the top of the trailer. The rope yanked and burned the handler's palms as the horse thrashed and retreated. Then Knox kicked up both hind legs at the dog nipping at his heels.

I unhappily watched as the horse handler with the now-dented ego and burned hands tried to deal with Knox by yanking even more when he caught up with him. But Knox was determined not to go into the dark and unfamiliar trailer.

Now, I'm no horse whisperer, but I love horses, and I understand how a horse thinks. So I intervened by suggesting we call everything to a halt and give everyone time to calm down. After awhile I took Knox for a walk, and we had a little talk. It did wonders.

Knox didn't get over his apprehension immediately, but I hoped he would trust me enough to eventually step into the trailer on his own. I calmly walked him up to the edge of the trailer and released the tension on his lead rope. I didn't let him back up and run away, but I didn't yank and manhandle him either. I gave him some feed, talked to him, patted and stroked him. I opened the door so that he could see his friend Nash. I even stood inside the dark trailer to show him everything would be okay.

After fifteen minutes of calm, Knox put one front foot onto the trailer. In another five minutes, the other front foot. In another five minutes, the third. That fourth foot took the longest and a slight pat on the rear, but Knox finally stepped up into the trailer.

Knox was nervous about the sound of the trailer's wood floor, and it was dark and unfamiliar. So I stood in the trailer between the two horses, calmly letting them know that they were going to be okay. We all calmed down together.

Patience, which the handler later exclaimed that he lacked, helped us reach the goal, but my success with Knox was not so much about patience as it was about technique, and giving control back to the animal.

Do you suppose there is any lesson for parenting a resistant teen in this story? You bet! At Heartlight, the kids learn a lot by handling horses, and sometimes we learn from the horses as well. Here's what Knox and Nash demonstrated to us that night that applies directly to parenting teens:

1. **No two teens are alike.** What works for one doesn't always work for another. Just because one is comfortable doesn't mean the other feels the same way. What feels safe for one is scary for another. It's important to know different techniques to handle their different responses. It's also important to ask questions and listen to figure out which technique is needed. Don't assume you know what a teen is feeling or what is motivating him. Ask him.

2. **You can't get a child to go where you're not willing to go yourself.** Hop up in that place you want your child to go. Let her know that even though it's scary, it is better. If your behavior suggests to your teen that where you want her to go is not some place you would personally go (or like), there is not much hope in getting your teen there. It's kind of like going to the dentist. We all know we need to go at least once a year, but most of us hate going, so we put it off and put it off, only going when the pain is too unbearable. When you wait that long, it's very expensive and

will probably take numerous visits to fix the problem. If you had gone for the regular checkups, the expense and pain might have been prevented. If you become willing to go to the emotional and physical places you are trying to have your teen go, you just might prevent some future pain and struggles.

3. **You have to learn to let go of the rope.** When you yank and pull, you create the atmosphere for a fight. You don't have to be in control. It is better to give over control to your teen (while still holding the reins lightly), and let her focus on why she needs to move in the direction you're inviting her, rather than causing her to rebel against your manhandling techniques.

4. **When something doesn't work, try a different approach.** That which you think must be yanked, pulled, tugged, jerked, and wrenched, might instead need to be lured, attracted, or enticed. Your push-pull technique might work well when making taffy, but it just won't work with teens (or horses). The harder you push, the more they will resist. Your tug-of-war approach could invoke full rebellion on your teen's part.

5. **You can call a time-out to regain calm.** If the situation is out of control, call a time-out. Go for a walk and have a little talk. Breathe. It works wonders. Not only will it help you get past the current issue, but also it helps to teach your teen how to work through conflicts, a useful skill for any adult.

6. **You can't take the steps for them.** Create the atmosphere for them to take steps, but don't do it for them or force them forward. Let your teen have some control. The sense of accomplishment and satisfaction that comes from negotiating even baby steps successfully is such a powerful motivator that teens will repeat the behaviors that brought them about.

7. **A gentle approach invites a kind response.** Your teen's hesitancy may be in response to the heavy-handed *way* that you are asking, not *what* you are asking. Relax! It's not a race. Let your teen set the pace. Unless it is a life or death situation, bulldozing your teen into a new response is going to fail, causing more strife and struggle.

8. **A gentle nudge at just the right moment encourages progress.** A gentle nudge can convey the message that even if your child fails, you will still love him or her. Teens often feel

that the love of their parents is conditional (and sometimes they're right!). It is sad that parents' behavior sends the message that they will withhold love. The message you should be sending and that you should be very familiar with by now is, *"No matter what you do, I cannot love you less. And no matter what you do, I cannot love you more."*

9. **You should not hesitate to stand with your teen in that new place.** It may be momentarily dark, and it may even stink a little… but it builds a great relationship of trust.

Many parents limit their parenting skills to those they already have "in the bag" and don't look for new ways of dealing with a resistant teen. Teens can be like those horses (and sometimes even as stubborn as mules!). Each is different and responds and learns differently. If your teen has dug in his or her heels and you are getting nowhere, you would be wise to seek a new approach. Sit with your teen, quietly wait for him to invite you into what is going on in his head. Don't make demands. Ask questions. Listen to the answers. Don't interrupt. Ask how you can be a better parent. Ask your teen what he or she needs from you in this situation. Really listen to the answers!

This give-and-take shows your teen that you are willing and able to release control, allowing him to grow in maturity and decision-making skills. It also helps him to learn conflict resolution and communication skills. After all, that is the goal of parenting, right? Equipping our teens to be mature, healthy, responsible and capable adults, of course!

How Can I Adapt to My Teen's Needs?

"Our son doesn't communicate with us anymore. Any time I ask questions, he just says, 'I don't know.' We always used to talk, and he doesn't do that anymore. We used to always have fun, and it hasn't been too fun the last year. What can we do to adapt our parenting to his needs? Please help us...we think we're losing our son."

Do you allow your teenager to make mistakes? Or do you protect him from that? Think about it—if you hadn't learned from your own mistakes, how would you know what it means to make one? And if you prevent your teen from making mistakes, how else will he grow into maturity? By lecturing him? By rescuing him every time? Based on what I've learned from thirty years of working with troubled teens, that mode of parenting simply isn't helpful to children in their teenage years.

Perhaps you recall the Biosphere 2 experiment that started in 1991. Several scientists were sealed in a huge glass structure in the Arizona desert to see if life could be sustained in an ecologically closed system. If it worked, it could be a model for what might be built in outer space. There was one unexpected result from that experiment. As trees were grown in this seemingly "perfect" environment, with sun and water and good soil, they all eventually died. You see, as trees normally grow in nature, winds continuously bend them back and forth, making microscopic tears in their bark.

The tree responds by filling the tiny breaks with protective sap that hardens and forms a sturdy outer core, making the tree trunk strong enough to stand upright. Without the buffeting winds in the protected system of Biosphere 2, the trees there simply flopped over and broke after reaching a certain height.

I hope the analogy to parenting is obvious. Are you overly protective of teenagers in your own "system"? Can you see how that could become detrimental, or at the very least not be very helpful to them, when in a few short years they will take on life all on their own?

After years of being in *protector* mode, we need to get out of the way and allow our children to gradually bend in the winds of life a little more. Through that gentle buffeting, they'll gain strength and wisdom to stand upright and flourish in their later years. Without it, they will simply fall over at some point. We have all heard of forty-year-olds who still live with their parents because they lack the social skills or motivation to strike out on their own. There was even a movie released recently called *Failure to Launch* about a thirty-something male who, despite his career success, refused to consider moving out of his parents' house because mom did everything for him – cooked, cleaned, nagged, everything! If you do not adjust your parenting techniques from controlling to mentoring and coaching during your child's early adolescence, you may just end up with a nest that never empties!

Your adaptation must also encompass moving from "telling and providing" to "listening and guiding." In other words, avoid fixing everything for the little darlings, but be there for them to cry on your shoulder when they make a mistake. Learning to listen instead of tell is a real challenge for most parents. For over a decade, you have been the voice of reason, conscience, and motivation for your children. Now you have to be quiet and let them start figuring some things out on their own. (And I know that after watching your adolescent boy stick a peanut up his nose to impress his friends, that may rightly scare the pee out of you.) But it helps their cognitive skills grow from concrete thinking to abstract thinking, which is very important. I would like to issue a challenge to all parents. I call it "The Shut-up Challenge." I'm not trying to be rude (I know saying "Shut up" is a no-no in some households.), but I am dead serious - just shut up! In case I haven't made myself clear enough, that means be quiet, stay silent, zip it, don't speak—at all.

"Even a fool is thought wise when he keeps silent," Proverbs 17:28, NIV.

So, take "The Shut-up Challenge." Try it for a day, and watch what happens. When your teenager drops a "jewel" on you and says something you feel needs correcting, just be quiet. Don't flip out, argue, or try to make it right. Just let it go. Stop lecturing, start listening.

You may be surprised to find that:

1. You can't do it. You just can't keep quiet. You are not a good listener, and listening to your child is an area you need to grow in.
2. Your child has a mind of his own and is fully able to use it without you constantly pointing him in the direction you think he needs to go.
3. Your child wants to talk to you more when you don't verbally beat him down every opportunity you get.
4. Your child has ideas that are different from yours. Perhaps he doesn't want what you want, and you need to change your mind about some things.
5. Your child may learn the important lessons in one teachable moment, and you don't need all that other verbal garbage to make your point.

"But, Mark," you say, "I can't teach my child what he needs to know by being quiet!"

Yes, you can - and most of the time you should.

For those times when you need to address an issue, I recommend trying a different approach. Instead of making your point, try asking a question. Not a rhetorical question either—that's just back-alley lecturing. Asking the right question may help your teen arrive at the right answer in a way that engages his thinking process and system of beliefs. You may be surprised to find he comes to the right conclusion all on his own.

For example:

"I never thought of it that way. What makes you think so?"

"What do you think will happen if...?"

Success in "The Shut-up Challenge" means you create a space in your relationship with your teen by taking a verbal step backwards. This will allow your teen to move toward you. Give your teen room to ask some questions of his own and come to his own conclusions. Instead of always pushing to lead the discussion or to turn it into a one-way lecture, you might just be invited by your teen to participate in the best two-way conversation you've ever had.

Remember when you were teaching your child to ride his bike for the first time? How many times did he fall before he was able to make it to the end of the block and back? Quite a few times, I would bet. Well, in adolescence, your teen is learning to ride a new bike. The "bike" of adulthood. He's going to fall down a lot. Be there to help him stand up again, brush the dirt off his pants, and push him in the right direction. Encourage your teens to make as many of their own decisions as possible. As long as the mistakes aren't life-threatening, it is OKAY that they mess up. We all learn best by doing something and then having to redo it because we messed up the first time.

Your teenagers may not get it quite right at first, but eventually, through natural consequences, they will learn to make better decisions. Begin early, and keep working at it. This is an ongoing process and one you should consider a critical stepping-stone to maturity. You and your teen will have missteps. It's not going to always be smooth and easy. The important thing to remember is that you can and will get through this. If you keep focusing on the relationship with your teen, you both will be better for it in the end.

You can adapt to your teen's needs by stepping back and changing gears from having to do everything and know everything to encouraging, listening and mentoring your teen in his growth and maturation. Take a deep breath and loosen you grip on the reins. Let your teen take up the slack and start making more decisions about his life – chores, job, extracurricular activities, rules and consequences. All of these need to be renegotiated in adolescence.

Parents of teenagers who really understand the shifting gears principle become really good coaches and listeners. They allow their children to learn from small mistakes along life's road in order to prepare them to handle bigger decisions later on. They remain in the game, enforcing the boundaries without wavering, but they avoid anger when boundaries are broken. They allow consequences to speak for themselves, for it is through consequences that we all learn. And they express true empathy and inspirational support during their teen's struggles, even when their teens make really stupid mistakes. They never say, "I told you so."

If you have a teenager in your home, perhaps it is time to shift your style of parenting. While it is hard to step back and watch as inevitable mistakes are made, it is essential for parents to allow the buffeting winds of life to blow. Give your teen some credit. You'll be surprised how quickly he or she will mature once the training wheels are taken off, and it is up to the kid to either steer straight or crash. Like the smile on a child's face after his first unassisted bike ride, your teen will grow in confidence and self-esteem with each new decision he makes.

Trying to understand how to help your teen in a world that is constantly changing is like trying to hit a target that constantly moves; just when your aim is right, things change—your kids change. Parents are often bewildered when trying to keep up with the always-changing world of teens. It's like trying to get a drink of water from a fire hydrant or hold a fistful of sand. Knowing how to set the right standards and enforce the right discipline can be overwhelming, and may seem impossible.

The key to success in this arena lies in learning to adapt your parenting style to be more fluid, more accessible.

As your child develops into a teen, you no longer have the luxury of making demands and expecting things to remain the same. Whether you like it or not, things change, and you must be able to understand and move with the culture and still set appropriate boundaries. I'm not saying you should stop caring about your family rules and beliefs. What I am saying is that how you enforce the rules must change. Otherwise, your child will be unprepared to cope with a culture that is constantly changing. He won't develop healthy relationships. Or she will remain immature and irresponsible, because all of the decisions have always been made for her.

Adapting your style must include learning how to set appropriate boundaries for their newly acquired behaviors, and giving them the choice of the direction they need to go.

A good example of how this works comes from the time I spend training horses. When I put a fence around a horse, I am setting up boundaries. The horse can go anywhere it likes within those fences. If a problem develops, I move the fences in a bit and reinforce the boundaries. The same can be true with your teen. Set boundaries, and allow your teen to choose his direction within those boundaries.

Properly set boundaries actually provide more freedom for your teen. Take the example of a playground surrounded by busy streets. Did you know that if it is unfenced, children will play only near the center of the playground? They are less likely to use the full playground space, because they don't want to get too close to the roads. However, if a fence is constructed around the outer edges of the playground, protecting the kids from the streets, the children will play all the way to the fence. It's the same way with your teen. If a problem develops or things change, move the boundaries in. Examine his world, and put some thought into what needs to be done.

Changing your parenting style for the teen years means you change your focus from punishment and discipline to training and character building.

The focus of the boundaries you set should become more about obedience, respect, and honesty, which are the top three qualities necessary to build solid relationships. Respect, more than anything else, allows all others to fall into their proper place. Think of respect as the cornerstone of a building. From respect grows honesty and obedience, as well as empathy and humility.

Encourage your teens to be involved in activities that are not about them or their performance – like volunteering at a homeless shelter, food bank, Habitat with Humanity—somewhere that will help your teens be respectful of others and serve. This will often mean that you or your spouse will also be volunteering with the same organization, so research and discuss the options thoroughly. If your teen has expressed an interest in medicine, look into the volunteer opportunities at your local hospital. If your teen loves animals, talk to a local vet or animal shelter about opportunities.

(These opportunities are often low-paying, part-time jobs, not just volunteer work.) There are many opportunities in communities around the country to help your teen get outside of herself, to broaden her sense of self, and to grow her in respect, obedience, honesty, empathy and humility.

Conversely, disobedience, disrespect, and dishonesty destroy relationships and need to be addressed when they appear. Dishonesty, more than anything else, destroys trust in relationships. Making your teen accountable for being dishonest is vital. It teaches your teen the importance of honesty by making them struggle through the hardships created by their dishonesty – loss of privileges, loss of possessions, or extra work to get back to the level where they were before being dishonest.

When your teen is caught in a lie, even after the consequences have been experienced, it is not an easy task to go "back to the way we were" before the lie. Your teen needs to experience that. Hold your teen responsible for the direction he chooses and cause him to own it, not to try to blame anyone else or make excuses. If your teen lays the blame on you, remember to put the responsibility clearly back on him. Tell him, "This is not about me or my mistakes, this is about you. I will never be a perfect parent, but if you don't change things, this will hurt you in your relationships in the future."

Adapting your style of parenting teens in order to meet the demands of today's world also means that you refocus your own attitudes and behavior. Make it your goal to:

- Move from lecturing to **discussing.**
- Move from entertaining to **experiencing something together.**
- Move from demanding everything, to **asking their ideas** about everything.
- Move from seeking justice to **giving grace.**
- Move from seeing everything that's wrong to **finding more of what's right.**
- Move from spending time always talking them to **more time listening.**
- Move from giving your opinion to **waiting until you are asked**.

It is difficult for teens today to grow up and move on. They tend to *like* their immaturity and don't feel the need to grow in their responsibilities. Teaching them to grow and *own* their attitudes and choices is one of the most important character qualities parents can help them develop. For your teens to succeed in adulthood, they will need to develop the skills and confidence to be able to own their attitudes, admit their mistakes, be open to constructive criticism, and make good choices. Adults who learn these things in adolescence are much more likely to be mature, respectful, and able to create and maintain healthy relationships.

So don't just tell them they need to be responsible, or that they need to be mature. Instead, carefully identify what is going on in their world, and begin to set out boundaries that give them responsibility and cause them to act upon it. And when the next new thing comes along, learn to adjust the boundaries in ways that help your teen continue to recognize the need to be mature, responsible, and willing to own up to the consequences of their choices.

How Do We Keep Our Marriage Going in the Midst of Teen Troubles?

"My daughter and I have had a strained relationship since her birth. She's been reared in a Christian home and loved much, but she has become increasingly defiant, disrespectful, and rebellious. She has become so angry that she disrupts the house. It just seems that everything we're trying just isn't working. It is affecting our marriage, as my husband is so frustrated that he takes it out on me. We don't agree on anything anymore. We always end up in a fight. It's almost as if her problems are causing our problems, and it's just getting too complicated. We're tired, we're falling apart, and we don't know how to save our marriage as we deal with this whole mess."

Recently, on our *weekly Heartlight Radio* program, my guest Dr. Melody Rhode commented that the death of a child is such a catastrophic experience in the life of parents that it leads to a marriage failure rate of seventy to eighty percent.[1] A shocking statistic, isn't it?

In my years of working with thousands of struggling teens and their parents, I've learned that parents of troubled teens can experience a similar sense of grief and loss, as well as a profound sense of betrayal, from their teen. Perhaps their teen has run away or otherwise has totally abandoned the family and everything they hold dear. To these parents, it may seem as though a death has occurred, As such, it puts a great deal of stress on their marriage.

Often, the crisis with a teen amplifies the true condition of a marriage, revealing its areas of weakness. A teen's acting out may actually be his unintentional way of forcing the adults in his life to deal with their obvious marital problems. It may be a relational problem that everyone in the family already knows exists but never talks about or addresses. Or it could simply be a lack of real love or respect in the relationship. Unfortunately, a parent who tends to be always absent or angry, too submissive or too strict, may demonstrate these traits even more as they try to deal with their teen's behavior. It can be overwhelming for any parent—and most marriages.

On the other hand, I've seen many parents (even parents who had previously divorced each other) band together when their teen experiences troubles. Contrary to the hopelessness of death, these parents are hopeful that something can yet be done to help their teen. They know that more is at stake than their own needs. They know that this issue with their teenager is bigger and more important than their own issues. Therefore, they know they had better get their own act together, or their teen may be lost forever. Having a teen spinning out of control is a powerful motivator for some parents to take a brutally honest inventory of their own issues and to begin working on the areas where they fall short.

For married parents who want to help their teen through this crisis, it is critical to understand that dealing with a struggling teen can be hard on your marriage. Really hard! And the failure of your marriage in the midst of the turmoil can lead to even more dire consequences for your teenager. To help you avoid these destructive forces, I encourage you to take these proactive steps:

Preventing Marital Jeopardy for Parents of Troubled Teens

- **See the experience as something you must manage together.** Attend couples counseling; get outside help specifically for managing your stress. If one of you tends to choose isolation from the problem or expresses anger inappropriately, address it with a professional. If you've never had reason or motivation to improve your relationship, keep in mind that saving your teen is a really good reason.

- **Begin to share your feelings about what's happening in your family.** Hiding your feelings from your spouse or not talking about your fears, anxieties, or worries only isolates you from the problem.

- **Present a united front to your teen, and insist that your child treat both of you respectfully.** This is a time when parenting comes from a love that is tough and remains strong, like that of a warrior ready to fight to keep a child from self-destruction. Treating each other respectfully is a first step.

- **Identify how your teen's out-of-control behavior is specifically hurting your marriage relationship, and express your feelings openly to your spouse.** Protect your spouse's feelings, and don't share them with others. Trying to guess how your spouse is really feeling is an impossible and frustrating task. You both must be open and honest about what you are feeling and thinking, or you can't work together to help your teen.

- **Don't expect your spouse to fill the void** left by your teen's wrong choices or absence. Your spouse is your partner and helpmate. He or she is not a substitute for things that are missing from your life. If you have voids in your life that you are expecting your spouse to fill, seek professional help to learn to find the appropriate way of filling those voids. If your teen has left you with this sense, only rebuilding your relationship with your teen will refill it. Nobody else can.

- **Don't expect your spouse to change.** Instead, focus on changing yourself. The only person you can control is yourself. Changing yourself – becoming stronger, healthier, happier – through counseling, spiritual growth, etc. will change the environment of your home. But you cannot expect everyone else to change. You can hope for it, definitely pray for it, but you can't demand it or expect it. That will only cause more frustration and pain in an already stressful situation.

- **Don't vent your frustrations on anyone else in the family, especially your spouse.** Find other ways to vent that don't include relationship-bashing. We have all come home from particularly bad days at work and emotionally vomited on our spouses. This is something you need to work hard at not doing during the crisis with your teen. If you continually yell, harp, blame, or bash your spouse every time you get frustrated or angry with your teen, you will just make the entire household more miserable. First, you are sending the message to your spouse that you do not love, trust, enjoy or want him or her there. Second, you are teaching your teen that it is okay to be disrespectful and hurtful to the people they love. Respect is one of the most vital stones in the foundation of maturity. Without it, no relationship will be able to withhold the storms and crises life hands out.

- **Don't blame each other for the trouble you are experiencing with your teen.** Blame will help no one at this point and, in fact, will feed your teen's problems. Blaming each other keeps your teen from having to own up to his own behavior. Without owning his own behavior and experiencing the full brunt of the consequences, he will not change. Your teen will simply not grow into the mature adult he is meant to become.

- **Find other parents who are experiencing similar issues with their teens, and spend time with them.** Relay your struggles and give them the chance to do the same. It may be difficult to find others who are willing to engage in such a private discussion, so be willing to start the discussion yourself, if needed. Attend conferences like our *Dealing with Today's Teens* seminar to help you gain insight and understanding that you are not alone in this struggle.

- **Respond instead of reacting to what comes your way.** Take time to think it through before you make a decision, and make certain the decision is one you both support. Ask God's help in finding the right answers and strength to do what's necessary. Face each situation as a team. Avoid knee-jerk reactions or making decisions without your spouse's input and cooperation.

- **Don't avoid the pain. If you avoid dealing with the pain, you avoid finding a solution.** Examine the feelings of loss, betrayal, sorrow, or anger and ask God to come alongside and bear your burdens. There is always a reason for the pain. God is able to use every situation to bring glory to His name and healing to His children. If you avoid the pain, you are missing an opportunity to experience God's love working in your life.

- **Make decisions together as much as possible in regard to your teen, but don't undermine your spouse's decisions, even if they are not discussed in advance.** Recognize that there are things your spouse will do differently, and let those become your strength. Try to support each other's style of parenting, even if it's not always what you would do or how you would do it. Be open. Your way is not the only way of doing things. The more techniques you have in your parenting arsenal, the better equipped you will be to deal with whatever your teen might throw at you. Have open and honest discussions with your spouse to discover creative ways the two of you have to work together to help your teen.

- **Build in some fun times together.** No matter how stressful the situation with your teen is, it's okay to still have fun— especially with your spouse. Blow off steam with regular date nights, a walk on the beach, a round of golf or other recreational activity. Laugh together as often as you can, so that when you cry together, you don't drown in despair.

- **Keep looking to the other side of the struggle.** Be patient. There is a light at the end of the tunnel, and it is God. Find hope in your relationship with God, and move in the direction He leads, knowing the struggle with your child will eventually end, and the teen who gives you the hardest time is often the one you'll end up relating to best down the road.

Above all else, know this:

> *Teens in crisis are experts at pitting one parent against another, creating a wedge in order to deflect attention away from their own bad behavior.*

At a time like this, be aware that you will be challenged with more marital problems. If you keep in mind where those stressors are coming from and also take to heart the steps I've outlined above, it could save your marriage. Parenting a teen in crisis is a daunting task for the best-equipped parents. Feelings of frustration and anger are normal. Communicate with your spouse. Take the time each day to speak your heart and listen to each other. Remember, parenting is not a "his" or "her" job. It is an "us" job. You both have vital roles in the lives of your children. You both have to do intentional work at building and maintaining a united and healthy "us" to successfully navigate the crisis of a teen spinning out of control.

Am I Training My Teen to Succeed?

"Our son, Max, has become very defiant over the past year with regard to our authority as parents, the rules at school, and just about everything in life. It is a continuous problem; he is the class clown and is failing most classes. We homeschooled him until the seventh grade and then put him in a Christian school until last year. He's now in public school, and it's a mess! We should never have put him there. He hates us, and he doesn't mind telling us so. He's lost interest in everything we have provided for him, and we don't know what to do."

I receive two or three questions like this every day. The culture has changed so drastically that many of the ways Christian families try to safeguard their children against the influences of the world are not working as well as in the past. In some cases, parents are finding that their attempts to protect their children are causing greater problems for their teens in the long run. It all comes down to training teens to be prepared for the world in which they have to live. Christian parents may not want their kids to be like today's culture; however, I am seeing more and more Christian teens who have been so protected from the culture that when they become old enough to have to integrate effectively into the normal teenage social structure, they can't.

And while well-meaning Christian parents probably don't want to hear this, I see some of these teens struggling because they were too sheltered through homeschooling or going to Christian school. If you are homeschooling or sending your child to private school, please do not take offense! I simply believe from my work with teens that some cultural shifts have posed some interesting challenges that these two settings have to address if they desire to prepare their students to be able to survive in the teen world.

Don't think I am against a Christian education, home education, or private education. I'm actually for it all: public school, Christian school, homeschool, Internet school, hard knocks school, and any other institution dedicated to educating kids. I mean it. I'm for it all. So please hear me when I share concerns about some challenges that are before all educators in dealing with the world of teens.

I believe that parents must train their children at all age levels. And while a portion of that training is spiritual training, there are many other areas of training that also should be addressed and part of a child's protocol to insure that they assimilate what they have learned and who they are into a world that desperately needs their presence. The issue that I am concerned about for every Christian family is this: The main purpose of training should be to get kids ready for the world they *will* live in, not the world that parents would *like* for them to live in.

Clearly one of the bigger challenges that may be faced by many homeschoolers is making sure that homeschooled children receive the beneficial interactions that are needed at an early age to begin the development of social skills. If you choose to homeschool your children during their preadolescent years, make sure you give them the opportunities for social interaction. If you don't, and then you enroll them in the seventh grade at a public or private school, you have just written a recipe that has "disaster" written all over it. Putting an overly sheltered child, unfamiliar with social interaction, into a school setting is like throwing him into a lion's den. And when he finds himself trapped in the lion's lair, for mere survival's sake he will do anything to engage and fit into the social structure.

When a young man in the seventh grade can't function socially, as evidenced by this family's question, he will undoubtedly resort to other means to find acceptance. In this case, the young man has become the class clown. Some people might say that he's always been a funny child, but perhaps he hasn't learned to control his humor or control himself in a social setting and is resorting to what he knows to do to gain attention. Any child who has not been exposed to a normal social environment will resort to whatever he knows to fit in socially when thrust into an unfamiliar setting. When all the "tricks in their bag" don't work, he gets mad. And when he gets mad, parents end up dealing with a whole different set of issues.

I would surmise from all the questions like this one that I have been asked, along with all the teens that I have worked with who have been homeschooled and sheltered in a secluded social setting, that this young man is angry at his mom and dad because they didn't prepare him for the world in which he was going to live.

My desire is for parents to train a child to enter the world that they will eventually live in. This does not mean I support or love the modern teen culture, but the culture is what it is. To choose not to train a child to enter that world and be able to function and survive is negligence on any parent's part, in my observation. Whether you homeschool, send your child to Christian school, or send them to public school, make sure you cover the cultural bases they will need to cross.

Here are some of the training areas I think are essential to be covered, so that Christian teens in today's culture can engage with others without losing their values and can be prepared to tackle the issues that are set before them without compromising their standards:

- Handling rejection and disappointment by allowing them to experience both.
- Learning a good work ethic that rewards a good day's work with a good day's pay.
- Learning to make wise decisions and how to work through the consequences of poor ones.
- Being exposed to the world to gain an understanding of it and how to keep its influence from overtaking their purpose.
- Learning how to make mistakes and bounce back from them.

- Allowing them to take responsibility for their lives and move from dependence at birth to independence by age eighteen.
- Helping them learn how to live in a sexually charged world.
- Learning about finances by giving them a checkbook beginning in the seventh grade.
- Teaching them some hobbies that can last a lifetime.
- Helping them set boundaries, say "no," and follow the rules.
- Teaching them about character, choosing the path of integrity, and encouraging honesty and keeping their word.
- Teaching them about commitment.
- Teaching them how to be the person their dog thinks they are.
- Teaching them how to have fun, laugh more, and enjoy and celebrate an abundant life.

To answer this family's question, I would suggest that these parents protect their son from his own foolish decisions. He will need counseling to help him process the emotional damage that will be inflicted by those he now has to engage with, and the family needs to "batten down the hatches" and get ready for a rough ride. This is the type of child who comes to Heartlight when parents can't get the situation under control.

My hope for this family—and your family, if you find yourself here—is that whatever they do in the days ahead, they will now focus on preparing their teen for the next steps in life: leaving home, going to college or getting married. I pray they will not neglect the fact that they have some catching up to do to help their son prepare to be able to function normally in the world.

I'm an avid supporter of homeschooling; however, I am equally supportive of a child learning to socially engage with the world that he will one day enter. If you are a homeschooling parent, make sure your children get social interaction. It is very hard for social "nerds" to integrate into mainstream society, if one day they must do that. Some kids would do better going to public school before they hit adolescence, then transitioning to home education for their middle and high school years.

Think this through with your children, and spend some time in discussion with them. Help them understand why you are requiring what you are requiring, and why you are insisting that they assume responsibility for some areas of their lives. In the long run, they'll appreciate that they've learned things from you (and hopefully they will pass these lessons on to your grandkids). Whatever you do, train your children for the world that they will live in, not the world that you want them to live in.

What Does My Teen Want from Me?

"My parents didn't give me much to go on in the realm of parenting. They pretty much did a lousy job, and I learned from them more about how not to parent than how to parent. Our kids are about to move into their teen years, and I'm afraid that I'm going to blow it as much as my parents did with me. Can you give me some advice on what teens want from parents these days?"

Years ago I listened on the radio to a man I've been a fan of all my life—Chuck Swindoll. I don't know what station or show he was on, nor do I remember what day it was or even what year it was. But it was early enough in my parenting and my youth worker days that I took his comments to heart. His words impacted me. In so many words, he stated this: "What I want written on my epitaph is, 'Dad was fun!'"

Does that surprise you? It did me.

I thought what every good Christian parent was supposed to have written on his epitaph was something to the effect of how godly he was or some thought about how spiritually he lived his life. And here was one of the most godly men I had ever heard sharing that he wanted to be known as a fun guy.

Years later, I heard Chuck Swindoll speak at a conference on biblical exposition, and I became more endeared to this imperfect man as he shared his faults, his wrongdoings, and his need for

Christ. I thought, "My lands, this man is just like me!" Then I put it all together and determined that I wanted to be a man like Chuck Swindoll—a man who knew Scripture, wasn't afraid to admit that he was a mess, and had fun with people.

I've been to many funerals of parents and have listened to their kids comment on their lives as they reflect on the years spent together. I've performed over four hundred weddings and have listened to countless grooms and brides get up before their friends at the rehearsal dinner and share what their parents have meant to them. I have had over two thousand teens live me and have heard their comments about their parents. I have counseled with teens in youth groups, camps, Young Life, and on mission trips and have listened to them share about their parents and what they mean to them. I have yet to hear any make comments like the following:

"I remember by Dad as always giving good devotions."

"When I think of my parents, I always remember how much they took me to church and Sunday school."

"Dad, I'm so appreciative that you taught me to memorize Scripture and made us watch VeggieTales videos and listen to Odyssey."

"Mom, I remember how cool it was that you made us always sit together in church, and wouldn't allow us to miss a time that the church doors were open."

"What I remember most about my parents is how they made me read my Bible, go to prayer meetings, and how we prayed together at dinner."

Now, just because I didn't hear those comments, doesn't mean no one has ever said them. Nor does it mean that any of the above is not important. But what is interesting to me is not so much what hasn't been said as what has been.

While I was working at a church in Tulsa, a group of administrative elders asked to meet with me to discuss how I was leading our youth group of more than four hundred kids. One man in particular, the chairman of this board, told me that he thought I wasn't spiritual enough for the kids in the youth group, that I had too much fun, and that I shouldn't share my life with these kids. It was at that moment that I knew beyond the shadow of a doubt that it was time for me to leave that church. So with a confidence that was probably a little too prideful, I thanked this man for his insight, told him that I was appreciative that he had acknowledged my success in reaching my goals and announced my resignation from that church.

A year later, I was visiting with that board chairman's son who was now attending college in Missouri, not far from where we had moved. He shared with me his struggles with his dad. I remember him saying, "He is the most godly but boring, non-relational man I've ever been around." Sinfully, in my twenty-seven-year-old heart, I was agreeing with him, wholeheartedly, saying to myself, *"I know what you mean."*

I have discovered throughout the years that the things people said they appreciated most about their parents didn't match up with the message I had heard in the beginning of my parenting years about what parenting was supposed to look like.

I really thought that Christian families were supposed to have daily devotions, go to church regularly, attend Sunday school, memorize Scripture, sing in the choir, pray together, give money to the church, sing loudly during the hymns, and not fall asleep during the sermons. I thought this was an equation for family success, and if I just did all of this, everything would turn out all right.

Then I saw families who did all these things, and their families didn't turn out all right. And those wonderful, spiritual "things" aren't the "things" that I heard people sharing about their parents when they reflected on what was meaningful to them.

The kind of parents I think teens long for today are parents who can admit they're not perfect, parents who will always love them and don't mind not being liked, parents who act like parents (not friends), parents who show character and integrity, and—believe it or not—parents who can say "no."

Imperfect Parents

Somehow, an imperfect parent makes a teen feel a little more human and not so messed up. When parents share their imperfections, a couple of things happen. First, teens are glad that you finally admitted where you fall short, because they've have seen it, and they are just waiting for it to be acknowledged. Second, your admission gives them permission to stop pretending they always have it together.

A young lady once told me that, although it was sinful, she felt pretty good when she heard that two parents we knew were getting a divorce. Everyone thought this was a perfect family with perfect kids, that they were all perfect people who lived in a perfect home. She told me that when she heard that this particular mom and dad had gotten divorced, she felt a little better about her own parents' divorce. She didn't feel like quite as much of an outcast. I believe this is a message Scripture has been telling us for quite some time: "*for all have sinned and fall short of the glory of God.*" (Romans 3:23, NIV).

As your children near their teen years, begin to share with them some of your downfalls, hurts, losses, and mistakes. That way, when they mess up, they will feel a sense that it is normal, that they're not weird or as much of a mess as people might be saying they are. When you reveal your mistakes, make sure that what you're sharing is age-appropriate. Age twelve is not the time to discuss with your child when you lost your virginity. But it may be a time that you share when you drank alcohol for the first time, if her age group is already dealing with that issue.

Parents, hear this loud and clear: Seventh grade isn't what it used to be! There are many discussions that need to take place during this adolescent year that in the past took place much later. Adolescents are being exposed to so much more so early on that they need someone to come alongside them early and stick around until the end.

Parents Who Love Without Having to Be Liked

Parenting adolescents is tough. They challenge you, confront you with your own inadequacies, and wear you out as you defend all the good things you desire for them. Part of the toughness of parenting is knowing that some of the things you say, some opinions you share, some rules you enforce and consequences you enact won't be taken by your teens with a big smile on their faces and warm "thank-yous." But your teens, whether they admit it or not, do like the fact that you're thinking of their best interests, even when—at the same time—they wish you wouldn't.

Drill sergeants aren't the most loved people in the world, but they're the people you want next to you when your life is on the line. A coach is not always a friendly person, but teens are sure appreciative when a good coach helps them capture a win. A counselor who shares some hard things with your teen isn't very appreciated until the teen realizes down the road that there was some wisdom in what that "idiot" said. A judge isn't very appreciated until the one being judged gets to the other side of their sentence. A true friend often gets his feelings hurt when he has to say some pretty truthful things to your teen, but they are wounds of faithfulness.

Good parents of adolescents perform all of the above roles. The parents who exhibit these traits have pushed, pulled, counseled, administered justice, and told the truth. Chances are, they aren't too well-liked during this time. But when teens finally see the bigger picture, they'll appreciate the role that these kinds of parents have played.

Parents Who Are Willing to Say "No"

Our generation of parents wants so much to say "yes" to everything teens request that the foolishness of teens is determining the roles of Mom and Dad. On the heels of reminding you that parents don't have to be liked in order to be truly loving and serving their teens well, I would tell you that it's okay to say "no" a little more often than you do. When you say "no," teens learn that it's okay for them to say the word "no." They learn that it's okay to stand up for what they believe. I know you've heard it before, but trust me, someday you'll be thanked numerous times if you can muster up the courage to "just say no."

Parents Who Are Parents First, Then a Friend

Parents need to remember that they are parents. Their role is one of authority, mentor, guide—but not yet a friend. Parents of teens need to be parents who are willing to exert some authority, who are not afraid to "put their foot down" when needed. Your teen needs a parent, and if you're not going to be that parent, they'll look for that role model elsewhere. They already have friends, and even if you think you're wearing the cool clothes, talking the same lingo, and getting in tight with their friends, I guarantee your teen does not think of you as one of his peers—no matter how hard you try. Plus, kids outgrow many of their friendships and move on to other friends. You don't want them to outgrow you!

There seems to be a shift for many parents to a parenting style that accommodates a teen's immaturity, and even enables it at times. Many times, parents who are struggling with their teens try to be their "friend" by becoming their teen's savior, rescuer, or lifeline. Parents who come alongside their teen and bail him out when he gets in trouble—in the hope of showing how much they love him—actually aren't showing him love at all. Love wants the best for a teen, and many parents' actions are far from the "best." Parents who try to be friends more than parents usually accommodate a teen's inappropriate behavior and thinking. While they may enjoy a facade of a relationship, most times it is only temporary because teens really want the closest adults to them to be ones who will do what's best, not what just fills the time with permissive recklessness.

Parents Who Won't Bend the Rules of Integrity and Who Have Character

Parents with integrity and character don't lie, won't cheat, and don't break their word. This is integrity, and parents who display it are the type of parents that most teens will cling to in their time of need. Teens know that parents with integrity can be trusted, because they have been watching your actions and interactions with others.

Hear me on this:

The honor your teens give you is directly proportional to the integrity that you display in everyday life.

These are the kinds of parents teens lean on during tough times. These are the parents who woo their children with the same message Jesus communicated—one that says, "Come to me, all you who are weary and burdened..." (Matthew 11:28, NIV)— and who, when a teen does come, do not administer judgment, condemnation, ridicule, or shame. Instead, these kinds of parents provide "rest." Rest because they know you can be trusted, that you'll do what's right, and that you'll keep your promises.

Oh, and back to my original story about Chuck Swindoll. I've heard the same thing from teens about what they would love to see in their parents—a sense of fun. So loosen up a little. Laugh a little more. Be a little more impetuous and impulsive. Tell a joke. Laugh at their jokes. You just might connect with your teen on a deeper level than you ever would have guessed.

QUESTION 18

How Much of My Teen's Business Is My Business?

"I feel guilty snooping around on my child's computer, looking at what he's been saying to others and where he's visited, reading his e-mails, and reading his friends' communications with him. Am I wrong to be doing this? I've taught my kids for years not to be deceitful, and I feel like that is exactly what I am doing."

In recent news, it was reported by North Carolina's Attorney General Roy Cooper that MySpace, the Web's most popular Web site for teenagers, is also actively used by at least twenty-nine thousand registered sex offenders.[1] My guess is that they aren't on MySpace to share recipes or to discuss politics.

I don't have to spin tales about how things in the modern world are far different from when we were teenagers; we already know they are. But what some parents don't know is how to effectively balance their teen's privacy and protection with their need to be involved in safeguarding their child. Do you have a tough time balancing your "need to know" with providing your teen some "private space"? For instance, some parents feel uneasy, as if they are being sneaky or are in violation of their child's trust, when they attempt to investigate their child's activities on the Internet. As one who daily sees the outcome of some of these cultural influences, let me set your mind at ease about monitoring your teen's activities, on or off the Internet.

First and foremost, I believe that a child needs and deserves some privacy, but he also needs to know that you, as a parent, will go to any end to find out what he's into if it begins affecting his attitudes and behaviors. After all, what he's into, or the hold an outsider may have on your teen through the Internet, may ultimately harm both him and your family. He may be too embarrassed to reveal it, or he could actually be afraid or feel threatened.

Good parents follow their instincts. If you feel there is something wrong, there probably is. If you sense there are secrets abounding around you, there probably are. If something tells you your child is hiding something, you're probably right. And when it comes to the Internet, more care must be taken, even if there is no outright cause for concern.

Get a Handle on the Internet...Even if Your Teen Shows No Signs of Trouble.

The Internet can pose some real dangers for teens. It is important to keep in mind that all rules for use of the Internet in your home must be adapted to the age of your child and his or her responsibility level. With that being said, here are some tips for parents to get the Internet under control:

1. **Make it a home policy that parents must know all electronic passwords.** This gives you access when you need it. Have access to your teens' social networking accounts (MySpace, Facebook, etc.) for monthly monitoring (or don't allow them on any network site if they can't be responsible). Add yourself to their "friends" lists to be able to roam around on their sites. Make their profiles private, so that only approved "friends" can communicate with them. A little monitoring goes a long way. If they refuse, disconnect the computer, have them take down their profile, or don't pay for their Internet access.

2. **Put high-quality internet screening/blocking software on the computer.** Maintain appropriate blocking levels on the browser software (blocking access to certain Web content, links or photos), and let the software do its work.

3. **Take the computer out of the bedroom!** This is the number-one safeguard for kids today. Even televisions, telephones, and cell phones should stay out in the open.

The more electronics your child has in his bedroom, the less he needs to come out of it and interact with his family. And the less you will know about what is happening in his life. At the very least, Internet access should not be in kids' bedrooms. Put the computer (or laptop) in an open area with the monitor visible from various angles. Don't allow access unless you are there. After all, would you let just anyone, including a registered sex offender, into your house to talk to your teen? Of course not. That portal to the outside world needs monitoring.

4. **Periodically view their Internet "browser history" and follow the trail.** You will be amazed; software is available to secretly record their every move if needed, especially if you think they are accessing the Internet overnight or when you are not home.

5. **If you feel there is a good reason to do so, read their e-mails.** Find out who they are chatting with. Watch where they go to "chat."

6. **Get on their social networking home page and look around.** Look at their friends. See what they're saying. Look at what is being said to them. Go visit their friends' pages. Listen to their music. Read their blogs. Read their descriptions of themselves. You might just find out something about your children that would be a perfect intro into some great conversations.

7. **If you find something inappropriate, talk to your child.** Don't assume the worst. All kids and teens are curious. Don't mistake a one-time look for a life-long habit. Be quick to listen, slow to speak, and slow to anger. You'll be amazed how your child will respond when you speak with a gentle spirit, not one of condemnation.

Please note that the above recommendations are not a license to be over-controlling to the point that you push your children away. I'm simply encouraging you to be proactive, which will hopefully allow you to avoid the regrets that come with not being "in the know."

I often say to teens, "Violation of my policy means violation of your privacy." If they violate my set house rules, including Internet usage rules, it changes what they can expect in terms of privacy. If they are dishonest and lie to me, I will seek, search, and look in areas I don't normally look in order to find the truth. If they are deceptive, I will investigate. If they lie, I will pry. If they hide something, I will seek relevant information. Why? Because, as a parent, I am concerned about the life of my child, and I am responsible for maintaining a sound and safe environment in the home until my child becomes an adult.

If your children are young, implement rules now to help keep you in the know. As your kids approach the teen years, update or add some new rules. Unless something in your teen's life is out of control or there has been a recent change in the behavior, mood, or school grades, then a parent should keep in the know by simply "looking around" and keeping an eye on things.

Tell Them You Are Watching.

You don't have to hide the fact that you are monitoring your kids. In fact, you shouldn't hide it. All parents must keep a "vigilant eye" on teenagers today. Call yourself an "alert mom or dad," or an "involved parent," if you will. Be a parent who says, "I will continue to be someone who has your back, even when you don't realize the serious nature of what you are getting into." Let your teens know that it is your job as a parent to keep your eyes wide open for anything going wrong, not so you can catch them doing wrong, but so that you can help them from falling into that trap in the first place.

If things are really spinning out of control, then it is time to have a "change of rules" discussion with your child. This implies that you will be even more vigilant about monitoring. Your teen's response will be, "You just don't trust me!" And your response can be, "It's not that I don't trust you; it's that I hope to trust you more." This statement tells your child, *"I don't want to control you; I want to be able to trust you, so use this opportunity to show me that I can trust you more than I ever have. I believe in privacy. I believe in trust. But I also believe in 'being there' to be the parent God has called me to be."*

When I am working with the teens at Heartlight, if I see anything that concerns me, it is brought into the open, shared, and discussed. I tell kids that I sleep with one eye open. I'm always looking for something that has the potential to destroy a relationship with them. I tell them that I'm looking out for them because I don't want any unwelcome thing to intrude into their lives.

QUESTION 19

When Will the
Chaos Ever Stop?

*"Are we ever going to get through this? I feel so angry
at God for giving me a son like this."*

When your teen is spinning out of control, it is frightening to
think about the damage he may be doing to his future. And that's
just what we parents do...we worry about our child when we see the
warning signs (grades dropping, hanging around with the wrong
crowd, drug use, depression, defiance, sexual promiscuity). The
unknown is always scary, but we cannot watch over our teenager
every minute. We also personalize our teen's struggles as a direct
reflection of who we are as people and how good we have been as
parents. This personalization often causes more pain and anger
within us than the current situation should cause. It's even natural
to be angry at God for what you see as something He controls, or
at the very least should have protected you from. I am not saying
that this is in ANY way God's fault. What I am saying is that it is
human to feel as if it is His fault and to be angry about it.

As an adult, as a parent, you need to identify this anger and
process through it before you can make any headway in the
struggles with your teen. It is okay to get angry with God. He is a
big God, a mighty God. He can take it. It is not okay to sit in the
squalor of that anger and let if fester inside you – rotting you and
your relationships along the way. It is not okay to take your anger
and frustration out on your spouse, your children or anyone else.
We have all done it, had horrible days and taken it out on those

closest to us. We love them and they feel safe to us, so we tend to think that it is okay to express any and all emotions that bubble up within us.

Well, it's not okay to take your frustrations, hurts and anger out on other people. This is where the boundaries of respect get violated. If you are trying to teach your teens how to be respectful, your actions show them whether you really mean it or not. If you respect someone, you don't emotionally vomit all over them when you have a bad day.

If you believe that God is behind your struggles with your teen, have you stopped to ask what He has in mind for you to learn through this struggle? Perhaps He wants you to grow just as much as He wants your teen to become a mature, responsible adult. Life is a process. You don't hit the age of thirty and say, "Hey, I've learned all of life's lessons. I can just sit back and coast for the rest of my time here." We are called to continually look within ourselves and mature in our faith and our lives. Are there areas in your life that you need to work on? Are you so frustrated with your teen because you see yourself reflected in her and really don't like what you see?

God can and will use any situation to bring glory to His name and to draw His children closer to Him. Is God trying to get your attention so that you will allow Him to heal areas of your life that you have been ignoring for far too long?

Are you dealing with a struggling teen in your home? Are emotions running high and hope running low? I'd like to offer you some advice to help you find peace in the midst of this struggle.

Life can be traumatic for parents watching helplessly as their child spins out of control. There are good days, and there are terrible days. They try this and they try that, and each time they think they've got it figured it out, their teen throws a curve ball and they sink to a new low.

I've found that the parents who are successful in navigating this storm seek God's peace in both the highs and the lows of life, as well as the muddle in the middle. They survive by keeping their faith strong, and they spend more time on their knees than on their feet. They let each day bring what it will, realizing that tomorrow may or may not look anything like today, and that in most cases, their teenager will eventually come around. "This too shall pass" becomes a mantra for parents bracing themselves through this time.

"Don't worry about anything; instead, pray about everything. Tell God what you need, and thank him for all he has done. Then you will experience God's peace, which exceeds anything we can understand. His peace will guard your hearts and minds as you live in Christ Jesus." (Philippians 4:6-7, NLT)

Most parents describe the struggle with a teenager as a "roller-coaster" or a "powder keg," and for many it can either be a time of the family banding together, or it can tear the family apart. With what is at stake, the most important thing you can do for your teenager is keep your other relationships strong and prevent the struggle with your teen from becoming the sole focus of your life.

You'll have those "valley" days. Walk through the valley, and keep on walking for as long as it takes. Do not stop to build monuments to your grief, anger, or fear. One thing that may help during the low times is to pull out old pictures and videos to remember the good old days when your teen didn't treat you like dirt. It will give you better perspective and strength to keep fighting for what's right for your teenager, even though it may be a totally one-sided and unappreciated fight for his future. Celebrate the good days. They'll likely be few and far between for a time, but that's okay. Let them prop you up. Enjoy each victory. Laugh with your teen. Reflect on the good, and hope for a future filled with more days like the few good ones you experience now.

Do you recall the discussion on consequences...how consequences are the best tool a parent can use to teach maturity? I mention it because God, your heavenly parent, may be using this situation with your teenager to teach you a thing or two. If so, take heed. Take a close look at your life to see if there is anything that needs changing. Most parents I deal with in our Heartlight residential program say that they, too, had to change before any real progress could be made with their teen. Consequences for your actions can affect your entire family. If you have a hard time facing fears and use control as a way to cope with those feelings, your whole family feels that. A consequence for an over-controlling nature is almost always rebellion of some sort. God will most definitely use a rebelling teen as a natural consequence for teaching you to rely on Him and not be fearful.

The bottom line is that parents can do no good for their teenager if they are caught up in despair and are constantly on edge. Learn early from others who have gotten to the other side of this struggle and actually survived! Give the reins to God, and He will give you peace, strength, and the right perspective to deal with your teenager. Look at what may need changing in your own life. And finally, no matter how your teen has hurt you, and no matter what your child has done, love your teen unconditionally, as God loves you.

What if We Don't Get a Happy Ending?

*"We had the perfect family for so many years.
Great relationships with all our kids and an overall
enjoyment in being together filled the walls of our
home. Then we found out that my husband had
pancreatic cancer. He died within four months. Two
months later, my son began to spin out of control
and became one of the angriest people I know.
I have been cussed out, yelled at, disrespected,
and punched by my son. Last year's Christmas
was wonderful...this year's was pure hell. I never
thought that things could turn so quickly. I feel
like I'm falling apart and beginning to become
depressed myself. How can I help my son when I
can barely hold it together myself?"*

When we first hold our newborns, their whole life and all the possibilities flash through our minds. *Will she be a dancer? Will he be a jock? I want her to do this. He needs to be like this.* As our children grow, we are able to live out those dreams for our children with them for a while. Young children are only too happy to do what Mommy and Daddy ask. Life is good. Your family is just like you always imagined. Everybody has his or her script and is following along perfectly. Then something happens – divorce, illness, job transfer, death, abuse – it could be just about anything. It could simply be the transition into adolescence. All of a sudden, seemingly overnight, everything changes. Someone is no longer following the script! Instead of this perfect family, you now have horror movie character Freddy Krueger at the breakfast table. How did this happen?

When you wake up and discover that your family is not what you always dreamed, the first question should be, "Is this really a bad thing?" Seriously, just because it is not how you want it to be, is this the worst thing that could be happening? Is your teen making decisions that are having a negative impact on her life and future, or are they just not the decisions you want her to make? If you are honest, and the answer is that your teen is making appropriate decisions, just not the ones you would like, then you need to relax. Your desire to control your teen and mold her into your dream for her will probably provoke her to anger and full-blown rebellion. This is not where you want to go.

If your teen is spinning out of control, that is a different situation altogether. If you can identify a specific situation that was the turning point in your teen's behavior, such as the death of a parent, that is where you need to start. The emotions wrapped up in that event are (or at least initially were) the motivators for your teen's current behavior. When something as devastating as the death of a parent occurs within a family, I strongly recommend seeking professional help to work through the pain and anger that come. Refusing to deal with these emotions in a healthy way is only going to lead to more pain and anger and a full-blown, out-of-control spin-out. It's not too late to get help!

If you are crushed by your own emotions from this event, how do you think your teen is feeling? Teens have not learned the skills to deal with all their emotions appropriately (especially the really intense emotions of anger, pain and loss). They are going to do whatever pops into their heads. Teens will take advantage of anything that is available, if they think it will help dull their pain – alcohol, drugs, sex, sports. This is not dealing with their pain, this is stuffing it into a box that will explode and take them even deeper when it does.

Recently, we traveled with some of our counseling staff to attend the *American Association of Christian Counselors* (AACC) annual convention in Nashville. Our friend, Dr. Larry Crabb, spoke in the plenary session Thursday, and he also joined us on our radio program. In our discussion, Dr. Crabb shared the struggle he experienced with one of his own teens and what he learned from going through that time.[1] Here are some of his key points:

Their Struggle, Our Struggle

Dr. Crabb reminded us that sometimes God sends our own children to speak to us concerning something we need to change in our own life, or even to reveal that we have valued our child more than our relationship with our Maker.

Lesser Things and the Greater Good

In the midst of the struggle and heartache, we should never forget that nothing can separate us from God's love and care. Stop "settling" for lesser things in life, and seek the greater good that God wants for you. If we could really see what God is up to, we'd be singing during those times of pain and tears instead of just focusing on our own pain.

Suffering and Glory

God promises glory on the other side of this struggle if we will commit our way (and our teenager) to Him. We need to surrender our teenager to God's care and allow Him to take some of the parenting load off our own shoulders.

Spiritual Companionship Equals Survival.

We should make known the struggle that is going on with our teen to a trusted companion. It is important to seek out a pastor, an elder, or a friend who is willing to come alongside us and literally pick us up off the floor, encourage us, and listen to how we hurt when our hearts have been broken by our teenager.

Even when it looks like you may never get a "happy ending," you have to survive and move forward in your relationship with God, the people He has put in your life, and with your child. Keep loving, keep learning, and when the happy ending doesn't show up here on earth, remember that you have the hope of eternity.

What Parents Can Do to Mentor and Guide Their Teen

QUESTION 21

How Do We Keep Our Expectations within Our Teen's Reach?

"Our daughter tells us that our standards are too high and we expect too much. As a result, she strives towards nothing. We want great things for her, but it seems the pressure we place on her is driving her away from us. Should we drop the standards to keep the relationship?"

If a teen shuts down her pursuit of reaching a particular standard or stops attempting to meet a parent's expectations, the teen's lack of action may be because, no matter how hard she tries, she feels she will never be able to accomplish what you desire from her. Don't get me wrong. The above statement, "We want great things for her," is a good desire for a parent to have for a teen. Most parents want great things for their kids, and very few teens that I've been with state that their parents want bad things for them. I don't think wanting your teen to succeed is the issue, but the pressure to achieve that a teen may feel can cause problems. And that pressure may be caused by the way that you communicate to your teen what you would like to see her do. Let me give you an example of what I mean:

I travel to different cities every weekend. Getting off an airplane and hopping in a car to drive to my next speaking engagement sounds much easier than it actually is, especially when you're as geographically challenged as I am. Directions and a paper map just don't mix as I'm barreling down a highway. To solve my issue of getting lost in cities I don't know, I purchased a Global Positioning System (GPS) that talks to me and shows me interactive maps as I travel through unknown streets. I've nicknamed this little digital compass Garmy, and Garmy and I head off to a new destination every weekend. She (Garmy has a woman's voice.) talks to me, shows me where I am, lets me know where I'm going, gives me an idea of how long the trip is going to take, and helps me get to the place where I need to be.

Once I punch in the address of my destination and let Garmy loose, she tells me where to turn, warns me of upcoming lane changes, points out highway exits that I should be looking for, and even shows me points of interest along the way. She's a joy to have and a blessing to travel with. Plus, unlike other backseat drivers, Garmy has an on/off switch for my sanity.

I've come to trust Garmy even when I don't feel like she's doing it the "right" way. I've learned to trust her when I feel like she's wrong. I've found that she always has the bigger picture in mind, knows of upcoming roadblocks and detours, and knows of changes in the path to my destination that I could never know. She's amazing…except for one thing…

Garmy always, always, *always* tells me when I make a wrong turn, miss an exit, or don't follow her instructions. She tells me in a condescending, digital monotone voice that she's "recalculating." I mean, she doesn't actually come out and say, "You've messed up, Buddy," or, "You just made a mistake." She just tells me in her certain way that she's recalculating, and because I know what she's thinking, I hear her unspoken snide comments and feel judgment, like I'm a failure, a moron, and one who is incapable.

In the heat of trying to get back on course on a few of my trips, I've wanted to chunk "Garmilla" out the window because of her demeaning attitude toward me when I've missed it. When I'm on course, she loves me. But let me make one mistake, and she dives into her calm "recalculating" rant. I know what she's trying to say, but anything good I feel for Garmy at times gets lost quickly because of that one word. To punish her, I sometimes don't put her back in her holder and let her sit in a hot car (with the windows rolled up) while I'm speaking inside a cool, air-conditioned auditorium. It's my payback.

Then there are times when Garmy redeems herself and makes me feel special. After weaving in and out of dangerous traffic and bumper-to-bumper near misses and following her instructions through a winding maze of highways and byways, she lets me know when I am almost "there." Upon reaching my address, she finally says, after a long and arduous journey, "You have arrived!" Why, those three words make me feel so significant that I occasionally drive around the block a few times just to hear her say it over and over and over.

Those are the times when she makes me feel that I am somebody, and those are the times when I put her in her soft case, place her in the pocket of my coat close to my heart, and let her hang out with me and my friends. I can be seen occasionally patting her just to let her know that I appreciate her companionship and value our relationship. Some people say that we have a co-dependent relationship. I tell people that, "Me and Garmy are tighter than a fat lady's sock." I value her, because I know, beyond a shadow of a doubt, that she has my best interest in mind and longs to get me where I want to be.

Understand the analogy?

Your teens know your standards and expectations, but sometimes wants to "chunk you out the window" for the way that you communicate those longings. Many times, the wonderful intent of the message gets lost in the not-so-wonderful approach of the messenger. Teens respond by shutting down, thus rejecting a great message. They hear a "recalculating" message that affirms what they wrestle with the most, the fear of failure and not being good enough. That makes them want to throw parents out the window and miss out on all the good those parents might be able to do in their lives.

Ask yourself, *"How do I come across to my teen?"*

I was walking through a hallway at a local high school when I heard the principal come on the public address system and express his disappointment in the students. He said, "You didn't cheer loudly enough at the pep rally, so I'm going to take away some privileges." I was shocked to hear that and chuckled as I thought to myself, *Did he really just say what I thought he said?* He evidently was embarrassed by their lack of enthusiasm at the pep rally, wanted to make a good "show" for his boss, and was willing to exert his authority to make sure that people lived up to his expectations.

A student walked passed me, and I heard him mutter, *"Man... what a dweeb!"* Isn't it amazing how a little string of words or comments made at the right time can change the perspective that a teen has of someone? The tongue has amazing power. The utterance of a single word, "recalculating," can make you want to chunk someone out the window, and the power of three simple words, "You have arrived," can endear one for life. The tongue can spark a giant, raging, out-of-control forest fire, or words of kindness can, as a rudder on a ship, turn the mightiest of vessels sailing on the ocean. Oh, the power of your tongue!

So, how do you come across to your teen?

Here are some potential chunk-Garmy-out-the-window statements that might put you at odds with your teen. Comments like these might just make you feel you've been put into a hot car with the windows rolled up when your teen responds to your well-intended (but hurtful) suggestions. Ever said anything like these to your teen?

> *"No daughter of mine is going to dress like a slut and go to church looking like that."*
>
> *"Honey, you don't want to look ridiculous wearing that to school."*
>
> *"You act like such a baby when you don't get your way. Why don't you grow up and act like your friend Sally? She never seems to be bothered by anything."*
>
> *"I wish you'd hang around some good friends. Those people you're with just don't live up to our standards."*
>
> *"You never pay attention when you're driving. Quit playing with the radio and focus on the other cars."*
>
> *"We expect you to be the best you can be and will not be satisfied until you put out some effort."*
>
> *"We know you can do better if you'll just try. Why, your brother made straight A's in high school, and he never put out any effort."*

"Why do you date guys like him? All he wants you for is your body. Why do you always attract the lousy guys?"

"I don't know how you can think that way and still go to church."

"If you quit practicing, you'll never be any good. Billy's mother says he practices all the time...That's why he's so good."

"Quit being so afraid of the ball. Just get up there and swing, and quit worrying about everyone in the stands. Quit being a chicken!"

"Why don't you get a job and quit being such a lazy slob? You can't expect everyone to always give you everything. Your sister never just sat around."

"Why don't you do something productive this summer rather than just hanging out with your girlfriend (or boyfriend or playing video games or watching television)? Your generation is so lazy...Why, when I was your age......"

"Remember, you're a Smith" (or whatever your last name is). Interpretation: *"We're better than everyone else, so act like it."*

"If you want to make something of yourself, you're going to have to go to college."

"Why do you want to go to that movie? It's just a comedy about stupid stuff."

"You never seem to date the good girls, and you always get stuck with airheads. Maybe you can find a good one someday."

"If you live like a slob, then you'll be a slob, and no girl will ever want to marry you. You think she'll want to spend all her life picking up after her husband?"

"No wonder you don't have any dates. You eat so much bad stuff and have gained so much weight; you'll never attract any good guys."

"If you use alcohol or tobacco you'll go to hell. I wish you could be like Matthew...He says that he will never touch either one."

"When I was your age, I dressed differently. I didn't look stupid. Do you not realize what you look like?"

"Your clothes always look terrible. People are going to think your mother doesn't care about the way you look."

"Why can't you hang out with the kids from church? They seem to be such nice kids."

These statements all reflect a parent's good intent, but they are communicated in ways that shut down teens, and may get a parent thrown from the car (hopefully not literally). These statements are offensive and demeaning in the way they are presented, yet the heart of each message is asking teens to reach for a higher standard or a greater expectation. They are messages loaded with good intent and bad delivery. It's like demonstrating the act of servanthood by washing your teen's feet…with boiling water.

Again I ask, *How do you come across?*

If you really want to know, ask your teen. Most teens, if they feel a response is "safe" and the atmosphere inviting, will share their heart about how your comments make them feel. And that which they don't speak, they will act out. The option is either to watch them act out their feelings, or listen to them share their hearts in a safe and inviting setting. Here are some thoughts on how to create that setting:

Don't Drive Yourself Nuts Trying to Correct Everything.

Constant correction deafens your teen's ears to your words of praise and adoration, and you'll drive yourself nuts in the process. Seeing everything that needs to change in the life of your teen, and thinking that it all needs to change *today* is a path that will push your teen further away from you and keep you up at night wondering why he avoids you.

Once your teens are used to hearing your constant correction every day, it's hard for them to switch gears when you decide not to correct as much, unless you announce a change in your approach. If you realize that you're overdoing it in the correction department, announce to your teen and the rest of your family, "I know that I've been hard on you guys, and I intend to back off. I don't want to be a nag." This statement doesn't mean that you back off altogether.

Rather, it is more about changing your style of engagement than giving up on the training process.

Remember, it doesn't do too much good to have a perfect child and lose the relationship in the process. I'd personally prefer to have a half-perfect child with a good relationship. The process takes time, and I assure you that you will have plenty of opportunities over your lifetime to give correction and further train, but you have to open the communication lines in a relationship for that to happen. If you nag like a dripping faucet, your teen will one day "fix" the plumbing—probably by turning it off or disconnecting the pipeline!

Their Memory Card Is Larger Than You Think.

Your teen is capable of remembering what you have asked them to do, the directions that you have given, and the rules of your home. In the same way that you don't have to keep reminding them of what you want for them, you also don't have to constantly repeat your instructions. And you don't have to keep reminding them when they blow it.

When I use my GPS and don't follow Garmy's instructions, I know that I'm off course. And since I already know it, I don't really like being reminded at every turn that she's recalculating. At that point, I usually pull over and mute her constant reminders of what a loser I am. There are even times that I'd rather not hear her at all, learn to operate without her voice, and rely on other sources to find my way.

Don't let your constant little reminders make your teens want to drown out your voice or rely on other sources to find their way. Their memory card is a lot larger than you think.

Let Them Know When They Have "Arrived."

Parents have got to let their teens know when they've done something right. Moms and Dads too often accentuate the areas where things are wrong or need correction, and take very little time to share what's going right. I can't tell you the number of times that I've had parents in their forties tell me how they never heard the words, *"Way to go!"* or, *"I'm proud of you,"* or, *"You've made your momma proud, son,"* or, *"You did a good job,"* or, *"Yessssssssssssssssss!"*

Don't let your son or daughter's legacy be that you were a parent who never affirmed anything positive. The words that you say today will stick with your kids throughout their lives. So make sure there are some good ones in your discussions!

Pick Your Battles Wisely.

Some people fight about stuff just for the sake of fighting. It's their way of engaging with people and having conversation. Some people like to fight just to show off. Others like to fight because they know of no other way to get people to pay attention to them. Then there are those who fight because they just don't have the good sense to let some things go, never realizing that the end result of a fight "won" at the cost of relationship really isn't a victory at all.

Parents can pick a fight over an issue and win—and be the biggest losers in the eyes of their teens. So pick your battles wisely. Age, wrinkles, and gray hair usually bring with it the wisdom to know which strike balls to swing at, and—here's the important, important part—which ones to let go.

There are issues that come out at the kitchen table, for example, that you know that you could hit "out of the park." It might be a comment made or a stance your teen takes that you know you could whittle down in order to show him where he is wrong. Ask yourself if what you want to say will be encouraging—or if you just want to be right. If you just want to get your view across, you may think you're hitting a "home run," when you might actually be losing the game with your teen.

Out of all the issues you battled with your parents, which ones really made a difference to your life today? Do you remember all those battles? The number of parent-teen relationships that were lost in the 1970s over the appropriate length of a guy's hair was absolutely amazing. The number of arguments we had around my parents' dining room table about the music of the 1970's (music that I now hear being played in grocery stores and elevators) was a waste.

I'm sure that there are issues today that don't really need to be issues. They're nothing more than a waste of breath and are a poor use of some good, and limited, time that you have with your teen. Just as there were things in your teen years that were a waste of time to argue over, are there some of those same items being "discussed" around your dining room table? Make it your goal to ask yourself before engaging your teen, *"Is winning this battle going to cost me the war?"*

Commit to Make Home a Place of Rest.

There are times when my kids and grandkids come over to our home that I prevent it from being a relaxing time just because I have a need to always be cleaning and putting things away. I follow everyone through the house, picking up, straightening up, and putting misplaced items back in their places. As a result, I keep everyone from feeling like they can relax. Here's my point: I sometimes do things to satisfy my needs and in the process keep others in my house from finding rest and a relationship-friendly environment.

I wonder sometimes why I'm like that. Perhaps I just want things in order. Perhaps I want to impress them with an ordered house. Who knows? Basically, my selfishness rules. When everyone leaves to go home, we've had anything but a relaxing time together—but everything sure is in its place! What a sad result, when what I really want is to tell people that they're welcome in my home. After all, I even put a doormat out front that says they are!

What do you do that keeps your teens from finding your home a place of rest in the midst of their societal and cultural battles? Do you get more concerned with the presentation of the food than the quality time spent together eating the meal? Are you more concerned with the celebration of the holiday and what your house looks like than the celebration of the relationships? Are you more concerned that your kids keep their feet off the coffee table than with them having a relaxing time with the "fam"? Are you more concerned with the cleanliness of your home than having a fun time making a mess together? Do you put off doing some things together because the work to clean up is just not worth the time spent together?

I feel like I'm kicking myself in the rear as I'm sharing this with you. I wonder...*Why do I do this?* Because I'm selfish. And my selfishness to create a place of rest for me sometimes keeps others from finding the rest that they desperately need.

Our homes are usually a reflection of who we really are, and our expectations for our homes are usually a reflection or extension of what we want for our teens. Why are some parents so adamant about their teen having a clean room and a made bed, when in the larger scope of their life, these two things are hardly of any significance? Yes, we want teens to have high standards and present themselves well, but when your mom used to nag you about your messy room, did it really make you feel fondly towards her?

I work hard to make sure that someone will not get up at my funeral and say, "Boy, Ol' Man Gregston was a great guy. He had the cleanest house I've ever seen, and it always made me feel like I was dirty." A stale and sterile home usually houses stale and sterile relationships. (And it's ironic to me that at the end of my life, as a payback for all my years of cleaning and picking up, my family is going to bury me under six feet of dirt.)

A few small changes in the way you operate your home can prompt some major changes in the attitude your teen has when he enters your home every night. With all the demands on teens today, home desperately needs to be that safe place where silence is golden, encouragement abounds, and relationships flourish. Your home should be a "retreat" from the pressures of a teen's life, not an addition to the pressures.

Communicating standards and expectations in a safe, inviting way and creating a home environment that gives off the messages you want to send provide an atmosphere that can create an arena for change in your relationships. If your child is saying that your expectations are beyond reach, don't lower your standards unless they are too high, but realize that you may need to do some "recalculating."

How Much Control Should We Give Our Teen?

"I think that we've spoiled our child rotten. Not only does he have everything there is in the world for teens (We've bought it all.), but also he wants us to do everything for him (and we do). He's the most immature sixteen-year-old we know. Whenever we're around his friends, they seem to be more responsible and mature than he is. What can we do to turn this ship around and get him headed in the right direction?"

Sometimes, parents feel that the only way they can be *good* parents is to be in control of their teenagers and prevent them from making mistakes. As I've pointed out before, that's not true. A good parent gradually gives control away to the teenager and helps the teen learn through the decisions he makes. It's time to quit doing everything for your teen. Think of it as taking a partial vacation. You get to let go of some of the responsibility you have been carrying around as a parent. You get to abdicate.

Don't get me wrong, you still have a ton of responsibility for your teen, but there are some things it is time for you to let go of. For example, start giving your teens more control over their money. Teach them about spending limits and budgeting. If your daughter blows her entire month's allowance on clothes the day after you give it to her, allow her to feel the pain and discomfort of not having anything for the rest of the month – that might even mean the dreaded sack lunch for school!

When a teen displays immaturity and irresponsibility or makes a really bad decision, parents are often too quick to snatch back control and clamp down even harder on the rules. In those situations, protecting the teen from making anymore mistakes may do more harm than good. Dr. Henry Cloud, co-author of the best-selling book *Boundaries,* has this to say about parents who over-control:

> *"The problem with over-control is this: while a major responsibility of good parenting is certainly to control and protect, they must make room for their child to make mistakes. Over-controlled children are subject to dependency, enmeshment conflicts and difficulty setting and keeping firm boundaries. They also have problems taking risks and being creative."* [1]

Handing Over the Reins

My best advice is to gradually allow your teenager to have some control, and avoid taking it back. The best parents do the following:

- Let their teens assume more and more responsibility.
- Encourage them to make thoughtful decisions.
- Set reasonable boundaries.
- Let their teens learn from their mistakes and don't soften the blow.
- Spend more time in discussion rather than dictation.
- Offer sound advice, *if* the teens want it.
- Avoid saying, "I told you so."

Control shouldn't be without limits.

Like training wheels on a bicycle, your child needs some control over their "ride" in life, but parents do need to put basic safeguards in place. These are the same kind of limits we as adults experience. For example, there is a spending limit on your credit cards, but it still gives you control over your own spending. Once you prove yourself, the credit card companies raise the limits. In every area of life we have limits, and it is important for your teens to learn how to incorporate living within certain limits as they make decisions on their own—before they leave the safety of your home.

The easing of control for an older teen might go something like this: "Yes, you can take the car, but you can only have one other teen in it, and you need to have it back here by eleven o'clock." You don't have to go into all the factual details, like studies have shown that having other teenagers in the car is a major cause of accidents for teenage drivers, and that most accidents for teens happen late at night. Simply make it known (and stick to it) that if your simple rules aren't followed, then the next time he needs it, the car won't be available to him.

Another example is expecting your teens to do their own laundry. This has several benefits. First, it's less laundry you have to do each week. Second, it teaches your teens how to do laundry, which is very important once they move out of your house. Third, it has a built-in consequence for not doing it. Once they run out of clean underwear a couple of times, they will be more consistent in doing it. Fourth, it teaches time management. Fifth, it reinforces all the lessons your teens have been given in how to follow directions. The first time your son turns all his white clothes pink by leaving a red item in the load will be the last time he doesn't sort!

Do you still demand that your teen keeps his room clean? Maybe it's time to release that area of control. There are certain battles that just aren't worth fighting with your teen. If you think your son's room is filthy and can't stand looking at it, start closing the door. Don't rescue your son when he runs out of clean clothes. Don't clean up for him because he lost a library book. Everybody has a "gross" threshold, and when your teen reaches it or has lost something he really wants, he will clean up. The control you give him over his "domain" is important. If he still has the border you put up when he was six, ask him if he wants to redecorate his room. Give him a budget, maybe set some color limits (maybe not), and let him do it himself. There's a good life lesson there. If he chooses poorly, he has to look at it every day! Don't offer to let him redo it.

A lack of limits has the tendency to produce a young adult who is selfish, dependent, demanding, entitled and aggressively controlling.

Teenagers will go wild if they aren't given some boundaries. Moral and ethical boundaries don't change from adolescence to adulthood, and neither should your expectations of your teen's behavior. What I'm referring to is giving control over more and more decisions about things like money, education, clothing, and transportation, not over whether or not it is time to abandon civilized behavior. Letting your teens decide whether or not they will be active in sports, band, and honors courses are some examples that can be very useful in preparing for college. They will have to decide these things on their own once they enter adulthood, so practicing their choices now will help them later.

These responsibilities and freedoms are not a ticket for your teens to do whatever they want. You still have veto power for decisions that have a major impact on your child's future or those that are moral issues. Will it really make a difference in twenty years if your teen participated in marching band in high school? Probably not. Will it change the future of your child if she decides she wants a GED at sixteen, so she can go to beauty school instead of graduating at eighteen and going on to college? Most definitely!

While teens are living at home, or even at college while you are paying their tuition, you can expect them to live within reasonable moral boundaries, or they'll lose some of the privileges you are providing. Consequences of breaking the established boundaries should be clear and understood up-front, and enforced without wavering.

Giving control to your teens means they'll begin learning by making small mistakes, but only if you allow those mistakes to hurt a bit. For example, if your teenage son takes his gas money and decides to blow it all on the latest iTunes downloads for his iPod, then you're not helping him by giving him more gas money. He needs to learn to set aside gas money and never use it for anything else. Softening the blow will only lead to your teen making the same mistake again and again. A lack of financial responsibility will only get worse until a much bigger consequence occurs.

Learning to be responsible with gas money or allowance helps equip your teen for the day when he or she will have credit cards and family budgets. If teens develop a habit of restraint during adolescence, they are much more likely not to develop spending problems with credit cards. If they don't learn this lesson because they are always bailed out, they will max out their credit cards, build mountains of debt, and be plagued with poor credit ratings in adulthood. Make it uncomfortable for them if they blow their budget! Don't give in because it makes you uncomfortable to see your teens uncomfortable. You will not do them any favors by caving in, not just on the financial stuff, but on any of your limits. Set your boundaries and consequences and stick to them!

By the way, your teen will rarely come right out and say that she made a bad decision. If you're waiting for it, don't hold your breath. In fact, she may defend her decision with all her might, all along knowing it was bad. It simply is not in a teen's nature to go around admitting mistakes, nor to offer that she was wrong. However, teens still learn from their mistakes, even if they don't always own up to them.

There are times in adulthood when we need to admit that we messed up. As a parent, being able to admit your faults to your child or teen is a lot harder than sharing them with your boss. It is so important, though. If you can model this type of behavior to your teens, you are giving them a powerful tool for when they become adults.

Also, take note of this once again: *Never* use the old, "I told you so" phrase with your kids when they make a mistake. If you're tempted, bite your tongue, because "I told you so" tends to undermine the learning experience (and it makes an adult sound childish, too). If you offered your sage advice (which is the reasonable thing for any parent to do), and they didn't heed it, then it is best to keep it to yourself. They may only 'fess up that they should have taken your advice years later, or when they become parents themselves.

When the time comes for our children to enter adulthood and make tough decisions on their own, we should hope that we have given them ample time and opportunities to learn by making smaller decisions. As in everything else in life, good decision-making takes practice. If they have had some control over their own decisions earlier on, and they've learned from the consequences of making wrong decisions, then we've done our job of teaching them. Our job is to raise well-grounded, mature, healthy adults.

Our children do not need to be taught how to be children; that comes naturally. They need to be taught how to be adults. Good decision-making skills are vital in adulthood! Just like removing the training wheels from a bicycle, parents of teens need to start allowing their teens more control over their worlds.

Most teenagers say that they want to be out on their own and make all their own decisions when they turn eighteen. The fact is, they usually have difficulty becoming independent. They secretly wish to avoid the kind of responsibilities they see their parents have for as long as possible. We may have to nudge them out of the nest in some way, and the best way to do that is to get them started early making their own decisions and learning to do so within limits. The more capable they are at making decisions for themselves, the more confident they will be. That confidence will allow them to take risks, try new things, and crave more freedom and independence.

Every parent wants to see their teens succeed in life. For them to be able to do that, they must be able to make good decisions. Allow them the opportunities to practice making decisions for themselves. Allow them control over some areas of their lives. As they consistently make more and more good decisions, give them more control. Let them fail and experience the impact of the consequences fully. Maintain your family belief system. Negotiate and renegotiate rules as things change. Enforce the consequences that you all agreed upon. Then, when the time comes, your teen will have the skills, boundaries and confidence to succeed in adulthood.

What If We've Done It Right, And It Still Goes Wrong?

"We've done everything right, but our teen is still
out of control. We have taken our son to church,
raised him in a Christian home, sent him to a great
Christian school, homeschooled him for a few years,
taken him on mission trips and poured our lives into
him. What has gone wrong? How can he reject all
that we've taught and all we've been striving for?"

The first thing that needs to be looked at is the statement, *"We have done everything right, but our teen is still out of control."* How do these parents know they did everything right? And if it all was right, was it right for them, the parents, or right for their teen? In this example, and in your family, it is important to remember that what worked for you as a child and teen probably will not work with today's youth. Their world is different. Do you consider what your teen really needs, or do you assume that because it makes you feel better, safer, or more in control, it must be right? Each teen is different. If something worked with one of your teens, there is no guarantee that it will work with any of your other teens. There is no "perfect equation" of parenting techniques that will work each and every time for each and every teen.

For instance, say you have two teens. One teen loves going to church; the other teen hates it. You react to the second teen's statements and actions as if she is purposefully and willfully rebelling against one of your stances – that family must attend church together. Have you stopped the demanding, cajoling and arguing to ask your teen why she hates going to church? Or have you just assumed that she was rebelling against your rules and therefore needed to be disciplined or punished? Maybe something happened there that hurt her, and she resents having to experience it again each time you make her attend. It doesn't have to be something life-shattering such as molestation. It could be that one of the popular girls made fun of her, and now she feels out of place. A feeling of not belonging in a church setting can be devastating to a teen. After all, everyone is supposed to be loved and give love in the Church, right? So your teen may rightfully wonder, *"Why doesn't anyone love me here?"*

Have you asked the question, "What is it about church that you don't like?" Have you listened to your teen? Have you considered attending a church of your child's choice? Maybe your teen just wants to be with her friends from school, or maybe that's who she wants to get away from. Is it acceptable in your family to attend different churches, or must you all attend the same church together? Could your stance change to adapt to the current situation?

What worked easily with your first teen may not work at all with any of your younger teens. Do you remember when you were a teen? Did everything always come easy and natural for you or your siblings? Even if you were an only child, you experienced things at home and in school that came easily to some of your peers and were extremely difficult for others. Each teen needs to be considered individually when it comes to making the rules and consequences in your family. Let each of them have a say in creating this system. If you simply try to create a bunch of rules and consequences from your viewpoint, you will be ruling over your family instead of preparing your teens for life on their own.

One teen may never need to have a curfew rule, whereas another may be hard-pressed to abide by his curfew rules. Taking phone privileges away from a boy may not have any impact on his behavior, whereas doing the same to a girl could bring about World War III. As parents, you really need to look at your teens—their likes, dislikes, learning styles, developmental levels. (Can they think abstractly yet, or are they still solid, concrete thinkers?)

Are the problems in your household all about them? Have they made some very poor choices, gotten into some real messes?

Sometimes it really isn't about you at all. You raised them and taught them good and strong values. Then one day, your teen decides that those things no longer work for him, so he will "try on" other values – the values of his peer group. He has decided that smoking is okay. That yelling at you is acceptable. He doesn't care that he is violating what he once believed in. He is not interested in how his behavior makes you feel. He is "in control." He can act as he chooses. Where's a parenting equation for this one? Every trick you have in your bag has failed. Your arsenal is empty. Did you do everything right? Possibly. The tricky thing about being a parent is that each of your children has free will, just as you do.

Children will make their own decisions and create their own value systems. The pain and stress come when we, as parents, recognize that our children have chosen poorly and are clearly (at least to us) heading down the wrong path. This is not just when their choices are self-destructive – drugs, alcohol, sexual promiscuity, and the like – but also when they decide to be the only Democrat in a century-old Republican family, when they begin practicing a different religion (or denomination), or decide that after years of playing piano and winning competition after competition, Julliard no longer matters.

That tends to be the hardest thing for parents, to allow their children to make poor decisions (or what appear to be poor choices to you), perhaps even to fail. It is all about your teen struggling to discover his or her identity and to become independent. It can be an extremely frustrating and painful process for all involved. You really did lay a firm foundation for your teen. You did a great job! You did such a great job that your teen feels so safe and independent that he feels it is time to create his own views. It may not seem like it to you at the moment, but that is a very good thing. This is how teens become mature, well-grounded adults who can contribute positively to this world. They are preparing to fly.

Sometimes it is hard for parents to let their teens spread their wings, especially since that typically involves several failed attempts and some discomfort, if not outright pain. No parents want to see their child fail or get hurt. Yet attempting to use the same equations and techniques to parent all of your teens can harm them – causing failure and discomfort.

Other times, it is all about you. Have you ever asked yourself, *"What on earth does God have in mind by allowing both me and my teen to struggle so?"*

I often see Christians who believe that parenting according to scriptural values, taking their kids to church every time the doors are open, and promoting family togetherness means that all will be well in the teenage years. Like buying an insurance plan, they think that doing the right things will bring about the right results. Sticking with the insurance policy analogy, why do we buy insurance? To help protect us if any unforeseen incidents occur, right? Car insurance is to protect us from the actions of other drivers as well as our own mistakes. Health insurance is purchased to take care of anything that can happen to damage or weaken our bodies. Do you see where I'm going? The things you did when your teen was a child were insurance. The problem is that insurance doesn't guarantee safe passage through life. It just helps protect you in case something does happen. The foundation that was laid in childhood remains throughout a person's life. Good, bad or indifferent, it will always be there.

Let me tell you, based on years of experience with struggling teens and their parents, the belief that you are guaranteed safe passage through adolescence if you have applied a strong, scripturally based parenting style is just plain wrong. Never assume that applying a continuous moral or religious presence in your child's life will, in itself, bring about a perfect transition from childhood to adulthood. It can help and should be encouraged, but it is no guarantee. The often-quoted Scripture, "Train a child in the way he should go, and when he is old he will not turn from it" (Proverbs 22:6, NIV) says nothing about the turbulent teenage years. In fact, you'll want to remember that some biblical characters with seemingly perfect spiritual upbringings had difficulties themselves in their teenage years.

You are still making decisions and behaving in ways that are colored and prompted by the foundation your parents laid when you were young. Did you struggle a lot during adolescence? Are there any wounds from your younger days that you have ignored, refused to work through, or need to ask God to heal? If there are, God might very well be talking directly to you through your teen's struggles!

Stuff happens that is out of our control as parents, and even if we do everything right, stuff still happens. One angelic teenager can lead us to think that we have found the *right formula*, right up until we see our next child go down a completely different path. Welcome to the real world—where God gives each of our children free will. And, welcome to the one thing in life over which you have absolutely no control. It may be the first time in your life that you have to lean on God completely. You know what? That's not all bad.

Could This Time Be God's Challenge to You?

In the heart of any parenting struggle, there is usually a lot that we can learn. For instance, could God want us to know Him more fully? Could we benefit from a different perspective and have a better understanding of how to help other kids or parents? Could this difficult time reveal areas of our lives that need to change?

The point is this: In God's economy, there is always a point to the pain. Allow God to use this time to move you to a better place as a family or to develop your own character individually. The whole purpose of adolescence is to grow. There are huge physical growth spurts, hormonal changes and maturation, and intellectual development in the teen years. It's not an easy journey for teens, and it is usually not an easy journey for parents. It can be extremely difficult for a parent who has never gotten beyond hurts that occurred during his own childhood or adolescence.

Are you the type of father who demands athletic perfection from your son? Did your dad do the same thing? Were you ever able to live up to his expectations and demands? Did you resent his attitude and quit sports, or did you stuff your feelings, take them out on weaker people (like bullies do) and excel at sports? Perhaps it is the mental and emotional scars each generation bears that God was talking about when He said that sins of the father will be visited upon the sons and daughters. If parents are struggling and limping along, children see that and learn to use those same coping techniques.

It is never too late to work on healing areas of your own life. Your teen will notice the changes in you. She will start asking questions, and with that invitation, you can share your new insights. She will need them. She needs to learn how to cope with stress in a productive and moral way. She needs to see that someone else's spitefulness towards her doesn't have to hurt her feelings, ruin her day, or leave emotional scars that last for years. She needs to see how to become a mature, well-adjusted, moral adult. If you don't have those attributes, how can you teach them to her? If you start working to develop these, your teen will be able to learn them, too. What blessings can come out of what seemed like such dark times in your life!

I know a lot of adults who think that now that they have reached a certain age, they no longer need to grow or learn. They either purposefully quit searching for things to learn and ways to better themselves, or they have just created such a cluttered life for themselves that all their responsibilities have bogged them down. There is nothing left in them. They stagnate. Spiritual stagnation can be very hard to identify if one only looks at the surface. *"I go to church every week. I'm on two committees. I teach Vacation Bible School."* Sound familiar? Where is your quiet time when you study God's Word, or be still for a few minutes so you can listen for God's will for you today? Do you take time for yourself to rejuvenate your spirit?

Consider Psalm 139:23-24 (NIV), which states,

"Search me, O God, and know my heart; test me and know my anxious thoughts. See if there is any offensive way in me, and lead me in the way everlasting."

God can't lead you if you are too busy even to do laundry! You can't see His path of righteousness if you are looking at everything your neighbor has that you don't. As adults, we have become very skilled at telling that "anxious little voice" to be quiet. During the day, we can easily ignore it because we have become so busy, but at night, that's when it gets us. We can't fall asleep. If we do fall asleep, we toss and turn all night, rarely getting the restorative sleep we need. We get cranky, short-tempered, and isolate ourselves. These are some of the "offensive" ways the Psalmist is talking about, not just big things like child abuse, committing crimes, or having affairs, but the little things that hurt those around us, even (especially) when we don't mean to.

In addition, think about Matthew 7:4-5 (NIV), when Jesus says, *"How can you say to your brother, 'Let me take the speck out of your eye,' when all the time there is a plank in your own eye? You hypocrite, first take the plank out of your own eye, and then you will see clearly to remove the speck from your brother's eye."*

Do you have something that needs attention in your own life at the same time as you seek help for your teen? If so, remember this...it could have lasting benefits that go far beyond this difficult period.

- You will learn to trust God in a very real way.
- You will learn how to become a good listener—one who waits to be invited.
- You will grow spiritually, become more self-controlled, slower to speak, slower to anger.
- You will realize that God is still dependable, even when everything seems out of control.
- You will learn the extent of God's great love for you.
- You will develop wisdom that is useful for the next generation in your family.
- Other parents will benefit from watching you handle your struggle in the right way.
- You will stop faking your faith and make your dependence upon God real.

You see, the struggle is always partly about us, how we handle things and how we seek God's help in the midst of the storm. Storms challenge us, sharpen our beliefs and help us confront our fear of losing control. Stated another way, this time of struggle with your teen will help build your faith and dependence on God's every provision in your life if you allow it to. The spiritual and emotional growth that you, as a parent, can gain from this time can have a powerful and positive impact in all areas of your life: your career, your marriage, your personal life, and your parenting life.

Aim Higher

Isn't it somewhat comforting to know that God may have a bigger purpose for everything that you and your teen are currently going through? If you believe that, then don't just focus on your teenager's struggles at this time. Step in front of a mirror and look for areas in your own life that need to grow, and aim to make those changes with God's help. You might not be able to make all the choices for your teen, but you can always make good choices for your own life—no matter how old you are or what you are going through.

Take a moment right now to think about how God might be using your situation to reveal more about His character, and how that knowledge can help you deal with your struggling teen. Learning to see the character of God is difficult, especially in times of struggle, so go to God's Word and study it. The Bible offers many passages describing and defining God's character and love for us.

Having teenagers in the house can be a scary and trying time for anyone. Isaiah wasn't speaking of raising teens when he wrote the following, but it is appropriate for everyone, including your teens, to know the following Scripture and believe that it is truly the Word of God:

> *"So do not fear, for I am with you; do not be dismayed, for I am your God. I will strengthen you and help you; I will uphold you with my righteous right hand... For I am the LORD, your God, who takes hold of your right hand and says to you, 'Do not fear; I will help you.'"* (Isaiah 41:10, 13, NIV)

What a wonderful and loving God! He is holding your right hand and is there to help. Here are other verses that are great to cling to:

> *"God is our refuge and strength, an ever-present help in trouble...The LORD Almighty is with us; the God of Jacob is our fortress... "* (Psalm 46:1, 11, NIV)

> *"Know therefore that the LORD your God is God; he is the faithful God, keeping his covenant of love to a thousand generations of those who love him and keep his commands."* (Deuteronomy 7:9, NIV)

> *"'Come now, let us reason together,' says the LORD. 'Though your sins are like scarlet, they shall be as white*

as snow; though they are red as crimson, they shall be like wool.'" (Isaiah 1:18, NIV)

Wow! God really does want to "reason together" with you, to talk about things, whatever they may be. He wants you to talk to Him and tell Him what you think, feel, want – anything and everything. He already knows, but He wants to hear it personally, just like you hope your teen will share information with you. It's about the personal relationship, the connection you have with your child. *"Come grab a soda, sit down, and let's talk about your day. Tell me what's going on in your head and your heart. I really do care. I really want to know. Why? Because if it's important to you, it's important to me."* That's how God feels, too!

Seek Him out, study His face, discover who your Father really is. In times of struggle, Christians are often quick to ask, *"Why have You forsaken me?"* This suggests that God has turned His back on us. The reality of the situation is that we have turned our backs or walked away from God, not the other way around. We have allowed our eyes to be drawn away from Him, to become burdened with fears and demands from this world. God is constant, unchanging and eternal. We are inconsistent, fallible and finite. Refocus you gaze away from yourself and back to God. Aim Higher! Then you will truly be doing the right thing, even if it seems like everything is going wrong.

QUESTION 24

What If We've Tried It All, and Nothing Seems to Work?

"My daughter has been arrested several times. She just ran away for the third time. She's sixteen and running with people she shouldn't be and using profanity constantly. She lies, manipulates, cheats at school, has mood swings, is extremely depressed, has no self-esteem, and rebels against anything, just to mention a few problems. She is currently running the streets, and I am unable to locate her. You name it, she's doing it. Please help!"

"Katie has begun to run away. She says she is not happy here and does not want to live here anymore. She is not obeying the house rules. If we tell her she can't do something, she does it anyway. She is not coming directly home after school. She is changing her friends. She is rude to family. She does not want counsel. She lost her mother three years ago and a grandmother she loved dearly a year ago. She treats us like dirt and thinks our rules are too strict. She wants to make decisions for herself about who she can hang with, where she can go and when she can do these things. She is now running away once or twice a week, usually to friends. We have lost control of her. I don't know what to do. She's seventeen."

There comes a time for some parents when kids have moved out, moved on, and really are out of their control. Even if they are not eighteen yet, some situations seem frustratingly out of parents' hands. If you feel like you've tried it all, and nothing has worked, what then?

Just as I believe in the redeeming gospel of Christ, the authority of Scripture, and the deity of Christ, I also believe in the freedom of choice. And some of the choices teens make move them into places where there is nothing anyone—even their parents—can do. I wish I could respond to every question sent to me with a resounding, *"Yes! I have the answers, and all you have to do is follow what I'm saying and everything will be fine."*

But that simply would not be true, for I know of many situations and crises where my answers fall short, and parents can't do a thing but sit back and watch as God does His work (even when it seems as if He is doing nothing).

There have been times that I have been involved with families when I have looked at the parents and said, "There's nothing you can do." Does that statement mean that all hope is lost? Not in the slightest! But there are times that parents must say, "I'm done," and trust God to do whatever He can to move a teen to a better place than where parents can take him.

Should you ever quit hoping? No. I believe there is always hope, as long as God is "alive and kickin'." And I don't mean that in a sacrilegious way, but in an affirming way, recognizing a living hope that is active and committed to making all things work together for good. He will never stop. It's just that parents, at times, must learn to trust Him and what He is going to do, rather than trusting that what they are doing to turn their teen around.

Here's an example of what I mean: Kristi was a young lady who was raised in a wonderful home, had two wonderful parents, wonderful brothers and sisters, and had a mind of her own. She wasn't going to listen to anyone else's directives, wisdom, or counsel. She was going to do it her way, regardless of the consequences. I met with her all during the time that she lived with us, spent time with her after she left us, and have continued to spend time with her over the last twenty years.

Her parents did everything to curb her behavior and reach out to help her through her struggles. Counseling. Belief Systems. Summer camps. Family camps. Family counseling. Hospitalization. Therapy. Residential counseling. Activities. Great relationships. Travel. Wilderness camps. Discussion after discussion. In short, Kristy's parents gave, gave, and then gave some more. Kristi, took, took, and took some more.

I remember driving through downtown Kansas City looking for Kristi on the streets as she prostituted herself for food and drugs. When I found her, she was pregnant, hungry—in short, a mess. She was hungry for conversation, for a familiar face, and for two London broil steaks that she wolfed down as soon as they were brought the table. I watched her eat as we sat there. She was so hungry that she didn't say a word. She reminded me of my dogs' response to me when I feed them—not a care that I am present.

I thought back to the time when Kristi had stolen my car, and I had her arrested. I remembered when she threw up all over the back of a friend's car when we found her on an afternoon that she ran away. I thought about the number of times that she had cussed me out, spit at me, and begged for me to let her do what she wanted. I wondered whether all my efforts were doing anything for this young lady, who I really liked in spite of all her stuff.

I walked with her back to her apartment and chatted as we strolled through the most pathetic part of the downtown area. It was really the only time in my life that I have felt uneasy and unsafe among the people we were around. We hugged and said good-bye, and I encouraged her to let me know when the baby arrived.

As I got in my car and drove back to the airport, I wondered, "How in God's green earth did this ever happen?" (an old saying I heard my mother use) I'm not sure that I knew what it meant, but it sure felt good to say it—to voice the sense of hopelessness that I felt. I wondered how God could have abandoned all the effort that was put into this young girl. I cried as I drove, feeling not only hopeless but helpless as I wondered whether there was anything I could have done differently or better. I was torn up. I felt lost. I wondered where God was in all the hard work, the trials, and this situation. I wasn't seeing Him, and I felt like He had abandoned me. And I wasn't even Kristi's parent! I was just someone who cared the world for her.

I remember her parents calling and saying that they had decided to "stop." They were going to quit putting themselves out and hand Kristi over to God, to truly trust God for their daughter's life. I thought, *"How can you give up on her?"* in such a vehement way that I found myself cussing at them under my breath and wondering how they could adopt a little girl when she was tiny and cute, only to un-adopt her twenty years later when she was a mess. I was lower than a grasshopper's belly and at a loss as to what to do next.

Yet somewhere I knew that God was still "alive and kickin'," and that He had a plan that none of us saw or even imagined. When we thought He had abandoned us, He really was involved the whole time. Hope never died. Our options did, but His plan never did. Behind the seemingly hopeless scene, God was preparing Kristi for something larger than what we all saw. Was there anything that any of us could do? Nope. But our lack of options was the beginning of His work in her life.

I know this. I *know* this—that even when I can't see God's hand in the midst of the situation and parents have no more options and there is an overwhelming sense that all is lost, *God has not abandoned anyone.* I know this because I have seen this over and over and over and over and over and over and over again. (Get my point?)

If you hit bottom as parents and you can't see Him, remember that doesn't mean He isn't there, isn't involved. Just because it's not turning out the way you wanted it to turn out, doesn't mean there are not good things happening!

God will not neglect His promises. Neither will He forget about His children. And one of those children happens to be your teen.

So what happened to Kristi? Just like her parents, today she is a wonderful person. She is now in her forties, has three kids, and is married to a wonderful man. The child she was pregnant with when I saw her in Kansas City is now twenty years old. Kristi's mother said that God used this "illegitimate child" to bring the whole family back together. Today, this loving mother laughs at her own doubt and ridicule of God's presence when she thought

He wasn't showing up. Kristi is now a wonderful mother and has a wonderful family...just like the one she grew up with.

I am moved to a great sense of worship as I listen to Kristi's comments about what God was doing in her life back then, and how He used everything that she experienced to mold her into the person she is today. She's commented to me that she thinks God not only allowed, but caused some of the "stuff" to happen in her life, so that she would be changed into the person she is today.

We all feel lost in the midst of the struggle...but perhaps we should be "lost" more often.

Great Story, But What Do I Do?

When a teen is as out of control as the ones described in the questions that opened this chapter, their issues are most likely not going to be resolved at home. It's time to sit down with your teen (if you can find him or her) and have the "talk" that communicates that you can no longer help, and that you'll no longer have your teen in your home. It will be a tough and probably emotional discussion. Letting a teen know that she is no longer welcome in the home does not facilitate a warm and loving time.

Parents have some options at this point:

I would tell the sixteen-year-old, because of her age, that she is going to a program somewhere, and that when she is of age, she can make her own decisions. While the legal age of adulthood is eighteen, most authorities I have talked to will not locate and transport a child over seventeen, should they be a runaway. Now this doesn't mean that parents can't place a seventeen-year-old child in a program like Heartlight, drug rehab, boarding school, or a wilderness program. It just means that they're not going to get much help from the authorities if the teen runs away. Parents and law enforcement officials' "hands are tied" because of legislation and legal precedence favoring juveniles. I truly think the situation is just about as frustrating for law enforcement as it is for parents as they see people in need and, in some cases, can't offer any assistance. Another option for parents is to use a transport service that, for a fee, will make a surprise early morning visit to your home, pick up your teen, and take her to the program of your choice.

Would I do this for the sixteen-year-old? Yes. I would continue to do what you can, while you can. At age seventeen, parents have some additional hurdles to jump to keep a child in a program, and at age eighteen, a child can do what he wants as long as there is no outstanding court order keeping him in any facility.

The cost of programs for kids can be another hurdle. It is expensive. I tell parents that programs like Heartlight cost about the same as staying in a mid-level hotel, except they stay at this "hotel" for about ten months at that daily rate. What they get from Heartlight that they don't get at a hotel is supervision, counseling, programs, activities, transportation, meals, schooling, entertainment, and family therapy. It's a good deal...but it's still expensive. Most people take out school loans, use up college funds, find support from churches or relatives, use insurance, use retirement or second mortgages. Families sacrifice a lot to make it happen.

The expense of such "help" is difficult for many people, thus adding to the frustration. Parents at first don't know what to do, then often can't afford it once they figure it all out. So if you have a sixteen-year-old acting out like the scenario listed above and you can't afford to get her the help that you want to give her, then you might have to rely on a probation department, relatives' homes, a friend's intervention, or allowing your child to move out and live with friends. Believe me, God will use everything in the life of your teen to "bring her back around." My prayer, as I'm sure it is yours, is that your child will begin to make some good decisions in the process of her prodigal experience.

When you have a seventeen-year-old spinning out of control and there is nothing you can do, you must make a choice about whether to have the child stay at home, wreak havoc within your family, and affect everyone's lives, or "turn him out" and let him learn what he needs to learn from the school of hard knocks. It's a difficult decision. I would encourage you to consider carefully how much damage your out-of-control teen is causing the rest of your family. Are other children being neglected or hurt by the amount of attention, time and resources focused on the troubled teen? I don't believe that any one person in a family is more important than the family as a whole. Additionally, I don't feel that parents should destroy the family and lose everyone in the process in their attempts to save one.

When your options are few and you've done all you can to offer something different for your child, I want you to know that God will continue to work in the life of your child when you let go. When you have exercised everything you know how to exercise, surrender. If you have an older teen who has the ability to leave home, your best option may be to let go, give your child what he wants, and pray that God will move in his life in ways that home has not been able to provide.

When you've tried it all and nothing seems to work, hand your child over to the Lord—your child's heavenly Father—and keep parenting from your knees. You can stop enabling but never stop praying.

How Do We Set Boundaries and Develop Our Teen's Faith?

"Vince feels like he can do whatever he wants and fears no consequences. He has no desire or ability to speak the truth. Our son is no longer accepting agreed-upon boundaries, is cutting school, smoking marijuana, staying out past curfew. Any help you can throw our way?"

When a teenager doesn't know what is expected in your home, he does what seems right in his own eyes, and that's a formula for chaos.

A good way to avoid chaos in the teenage years is to establish what I call a "Belief System for Discipline," a clear and undeniable plan for what is expected in your home. The root of the word *discipline* is "disciple," and discipline for your teen is best characterized by positive training or discipling, just as we saw Christ demonstrate with his disciples. A Belief System for Discipline is all about positive training and reinforcement of dearly held beliefs, including the consequences to expect if the rules are broken or boundaries crossed.

Having a clearly defined Belief System for your home helps everyone know how to act and where the "line" is that shouldn't be crossed. That way, kids know upfront what consequences to expect when they cross it. Teenagers can learn from established rules and consequences, but generally get frustrated when rules and consequences seem arbitrary or inconsistent.

Why is this so important? Because teens are prone to test their parents in every possible way. It is part of their built-in and growing need for independence, and they need to exercise their own free will. Parents need to take time to establish a clearly defined Belief System before their children enter the adolescent years. Doing so will go a long way toward avoiding parenting chaos and helping your teen eventually establish similar beliefs for himself.

A Belief System for Discipline is a set of beliefs, boundaries, rules, and consequences that governs the discipline in your home and remedies the chaos. Relief from chaos can only come when a cohesive Belief System is communicated in advance, and everyone knows what to expect. It lends a sense of security to highly insecure teenagers—especially when it comes to discipline. In other words, they know in advance whether or not experiencing the consequences is worth it when they are tempted to step across established boundaries.

I realize that some parents face insurmountable obstacles that come when a child spends time alternating between two sets of parents and two different sets of beliefs. This can be very difficult and confusing for everyone involved. Whenever possible, it is helpful for these sets of parents to think about uniting, whenever possible, under the banner of one Belief System for the sake of their children. Having two different systems is not impossible to work with, but it is much more difficult on everyone when two systems exist.

Your teenager may not agree with your Belief System for Discipline. He may not like it and may try to change your mind, but he cannot justify his misbehavior or avoid the consequences based on a difference of opinion. He knows well in advance what will happen if he transgresses the household Belief System, and can only hold himself responsible for the resulting consequences. It is important to state here that this Belief System needs to be discussed openly with all members of your family.

As parents, you are in charge, but open communication is a must. Be open to what your teens have to say. Consider their input. Some of your beliefs may need to be reevaluated. For instance, if you still hold the belief that teens should not have cell phones, you might (just might) want to reconsider that. In today's society, we have become accustomed to instant access to everyone. Not being able to contact your children, or them not being able to contact you, may need to be rethought. The world is constantly changing, and, as parents, we all need to adapt. I am not saying that foundational beliefs – the ones that really define who you are as a family – need to be changed.

For example, let's say that one aspect of your Belief System is that you believe smoking is bad for your health; therefore, smoking is not allowed in your home. Your teenager may not believe the same way, but it doesn't matter because this is your home, and this is what you believe. That belief will probably not change, even when your kids are adults. So you set a consequence for crossing that boundary. Your teenager then needs to decide for himself whether or not to smoke - and suffer the consequences if he chooses to do so.

Generational Beliefs—Family Background and Traditions

It's a given that the source of your Belief System for Discipline starts with you, your spouse, and the way you were both raised. You probably will not operate your home in exactly the same way as your parents. But you may adopt for your own home some of the same basic ideals you grew up with.

A simple example is the annual family vacation. Yes, that can be a part of your Belief System. If your parents provided for time away with the family on a yearly basis and it worked out well for you, then you will probably establish in your own Belief System that an annual family vacation is important as well. Or, if your parents believed it was best to teach you responsibility by allowing you to work for the things you wanted, you may likewise believe it's best for your children to work for the things they want. These are generational beliefs, traditions passed down from grandparent to parent to child.

As you build your Belief System, think about which aspects really worked in your childhood and your spouse's childhood. Can those beliefs work in your family now, or do they need to be adapted to be appropriate today or discarded completely? You and your spouse have to be honest about your childhoods. A lot of adults want to remember everything as being nice and fun as a child, but did the rule that every child plays sports really work for you? Did you like playing football, or would you have preferred to try art? If every child had to play the piano in your family, did that really make you happy, or did you want to do gymnastics? Please don't incorporate a belief into your Belief System that made you miserable simply because it is "what kids should do," and it was how you were raised. If it made you miserable and had no positive impact on your adult life, toss it! If you were miserable being forced to play sports, you will be miserable forcing your kids to play. Why? Because you can relate, and you have to drive them to all their games and practices, reliving your misery each time, as well as seeing theirs! Some traditions are really best left in the past.

Spiritual Beliefs—Character and Spiritual Walk

The next place to identify your beliefs, of course, is your relationship with God. The Bible is full of training on how to live honorably and in harmony with both God and man. The Bible is the best resource for ushering God's ideals for your home into your discipline structure. These are spiritual beliefs that address your child's character, spiritual training, and how you'll manage issues like honesty, obedience, and respect.

This section can be very difficult for people who have not consciously thought out their belief in God. We each have our own idea of who and what God is. Sometimes it is just a vague, blurry notion in the back of our minds. Sometimes it is a very clear, vibrant picture. As you think out your Belief System for Discipline using your spiritual beliefs, your concept of God can become clearer. Respect, honesty and obedience are cornerstones for spiritual behavior. From them grow empathy, humility and love.

As yourself these questions. Do you believe that your family should go to church every Sunday? Do you believe that you need to sit together in the worship service? Would you allow your kids to attend a different church if that's where their friends went to church? Are you going to make your teens go to youth group? Bible Study? Sing in the choir? Would you ever give an option for your teen to choose whether to go to church or not? What do you think that your teen needs to wear to church? Do you believe that your teen needs to give some of his/her money to church? What do you think you would tell your daughter if she said she wasn't going to church anymore? What would you tell your son if he skips out of Sunday School? Are you ready to allow your teen to make some decisions about their spiritual life?

Just asking questions to provoke a little thought.

Functional Beliefs—Your Unique Likes and Dislikes

Functional beliefs relate to everyday living, like how often bedrooms need to be cleaned in order to avert inspection by local health officials. Functional beliefs include whether chores are a part of each family member's duty in the home and must be done before anything else and whether you believe a good way to encourage your children in sports is to attend as many of their games as possible. These are functional beliefs, and they address the daily habits and quirks unique to each individual in the family.

If you have not already started working on a Belief System of Discipline, you should start now. Take time to write down some of your own generational, spiritual, and functional beliefs. You and your spouse should each make your own lists. Think about why you believe them and why they are important to you. After completing your individual lists, sit down and discuss them. If there are some beliefs that are poles apart, discuss them. Can a compromise be reached? Once you understand what you truly believe should be happening in your home, you will have the basis for moving toward the next step, which is to create and implement some healthy boundaries, rules, and consequences.

Establishing Boundaries

As discussed above, the first step in developing a Belief System for Discipline for your home is to identify your basic beliefs. The next important step to avoid family chaos is to evaluate your personal boundaries and how they relate to your beliefs. Boundaries define you. They are the fence posts placed around your behavior, or the delineation of how your beliefs are to be lived out. They are the "I will" and "I will not" statements that are the basis of your daily living and interaction with others. When they are defined, they help everyone in the family take responsibility for his own behavior, make his own choices, and know if he is headed into dangerous territory.

If an important cornerstone of your Belief System is *honesty*, then an umbrella family *boundary* in that regard could be: *We will be honest, and we will expect everyone in our family to be honest.*

For example, consider something gained dishonestly. What does your family do when a cashier returns too much change? Do you make it right, or do you keep the change? How about when something of value is found in a parking lot? Do you keep it or take it to the lost-and-found department? If you believe in honesty, your boundary is to seek to live honestly at all times. It is a clear line that is not to be crossed, even by keeping a lost or dishonestly gained item. It also means you will not accept dishonesty from others in your relationships.

Another good example of a boundary that supports the same belief in **honesty** might be: *I will seek to honestly admit my mistakes and make things right whenever possible.* That means, for example, that if I ding another's car in a parking lot, I'll leave my name and phone number if the other driver cannot be found. I will not just drive away and pretend it didn't happen.

Boundaries ensure family members take responsibility for themselves and their own actions.

A second example might be if you believe that *respect* for one another has merit, then your boundary will include showing respect to those you live with and teaching family members to respect those outside the family as well. Being respectful means not taking things without asking, not talking badly about another, not leaving a mess, not calling names or mouthing off. On the positive side, being respectful means celebrating each other's successes, helping each other out when needed, asking permission before using something that is not yours, or standing up for other family members. You fill in what you consider to be respectful and disrespectful practices.

Boundaries help us set thoughtful limits to our own behavior, ensuring right behavior in the heat of the moment.

As a final example, perhaps you believe that *dinnertime* is an important time for building family togetherness. A *boundary* in that regard could be: *I will plan and implement dinner for the family every evening and expect family members to be there whenever possible.* Creating a rule ahead of time that goes along with your belief and boundary alleviates future frustration: *No one is to make conflicting plans for dinnertime, nor accept phone calls or visits from friends during that time.*

Boundaries are about every member of the family, not just about you or your teen. They help us learn when to lovingly say "yes" or "no" when someone or something wants our time, our energy, our money, or our attention.

Boundaries are simply limits set around behavior to try to change the direction a child (or parent or family) is going. They define what you will and won't accept and should come from what you believe is right for your teen at this stage in his life and for your family.

When boundaries are crossed, it can be tough to take. It is never an easy enlightenment to find out that your teen has been doing things that are hardly acceptable, and it can be completely devastating when the truth comes out. Most parents are appalled. They just "can't believe" that their child would "ever do such a thing."

Consider the letter I received just the other day…

Saturday night, our 15-year old son informed us he felt guilty because he has been smoking pot and lying about it for the last six months. He confessed to our assistant pastor, a man he respects. The pastor encouraged our son to tell us. As you can well imagine, this has been quite a blow. My heart has been broken. I can't stop crying. I never, ever thought I'd go down this road with him. We agree our son needs discipline, but I fear my husband will be too harsh, and it will cause my son to further rebel. What is the right thing to do here?

In this situation, a family's boundaries have obviously been crossed by their teen—even if they were never openly discussed. Their teen knows he was breaking the law, and that is an obvious boundary.

The first thing parents should do in this suggestion is try to discern if they are dealing with just an ice cube, or if they have just touched the tip of an iceberg. In this scenario, the parents have many things working in their favor in dealing with their son, including:

- He confessed, so they didn't have to "find it out" or make any new discoveries.
- He said he feels guilty about what he was doing.
- He respects someone outside the family and felt comfortable telling that person, then his parents.
- He has a foundation of scriptural principles regarding his character.

Parents are doing the right thing to get a handle on the issue, and they are wise to carefully consider the discipline that they are about to take. But if you find yourself in a similar parenting situation, here's something to think about before you discipline: Discipline in its negative form, such as taking away privileges or possessions, is good, but taking away something won't always solve the problem entirely. It is only half of the solution for a teenager who wants to also be treated more like an adult, not a child.

Remember that smoking pot may be an attempt to numb any hurt he is feeling. When he is using drugs, the hurt temporarily goes away. Don't add to his pain by going overboard with the discipline you hand down or by telling him how disappointed you are in him. Fortifying your household boundaries, adding some new healthy boundaries, and strengthening your relationship will provide better results.

Boundaries include what your son already knows, what you've taught him all his life. They are the reason he is feeling guilty about smoking pot. But sometimes teens get confused over which boundaries are "childhood" boundaries and which are lifelong boundaries. For instance, holding mom's hand as you walk across the street is a childhood boundary. Avoiding illegal or immoral activity is a lifelong boundary. The goal for parents, then, is to make it clear to your teen which boundaries are appropriate for him now, according to the values you hold dear and plain, old common sense. (You may have noticed that teens don't always have a lot of common sense.)

Some healthy new boundaries could also include requiring your son to meet regularly with your assistant pastor, a good influence that he respects. Call and ask if he is willing to meet with your son for the next six weeks in order to talk through any underlying issues that are fueling his behavior or the feelings that led him to try pot in the first place. Tell your son you expect him to participate fully and that during this time you will limit his other activities and contact with friends, specifically those who encourage or participate in smoking pot.

Another positive boundary is to tell him that you will be testing him for drug use at home, using simple urine tests that you can buy at your local pharmacy. Tell him that any positive signs of drug use will result in a further plan of action. Knowing you'll test him for drugs periodically will help him avoid the pressure of using pot (or worse) when he is with friends or at school. In other words, he'll be able to say to them, "I can't, because my parents are testing me, and I'll be in real trouble if the test comes out positive."

As you develop healthy boundaries, make it a point (mom *and* dad) to spend time with your son on a regularly scheduled basis. Set up a weekly breakfast or dinner with just him. Be sure to mostly listen, not talk. Begin and end your discussion by reassuring him that *there is nothing he can do to make you love him more, and there's nothing he can do to make you love him less.* Don't be afraid to ask him the hard questions. Your goal should be to establish a solid relationship and encourage ongoing discussions.

As a result, other things he is struggling with may be revealed. Often, a teen is acting out due to deeper issues. Is he struggling with his sexuality? Are bullies threatening him at school? Does he feel intimidated by his peers into doing the wrong things they are doing? Could he be struggling with depression or low self-esteem? Ask him if he needs your help or the help of anyone else. Seek professional help if needed.

The bottom line is to avoid lecturing and begin listening and observing. Teenagers simply don't respond to lecturing, and it may take awhile for them to open up to you, but keep trying. Don't let the disappointment you feel cause you to pass judgment or condemn him, because he probably already feels badly enough, even if he doesn't outwardly show it.

Remember, this isn't about you, your reputation, or your parenting skills. It is about him. Move from disappointment and judgment to compassion, but make it clear what the boundaries are.

Take advantage of the opportunity before you to keep the relationship open and alive. Stand your ground concerning the boundaries and add some new boundaries, if needed, but strive to get through it all with your relationship intact. Then your son will learn to respect the healthy boundaries you've put into place in his life, and in the future will continue to come to you whenever he is struggling.

Sometimes boundaries need to be adjusted as your family grows up, in order to be more age-appropriate, or they may need to be honed to address a specific problem. Boundaries are not *rules.* Boundaries apply more to the person and how you will function within your relationships. They help you and your family take responsibility for your choices, and empower you all to set limits with others. You and your spouse should pick your top ten or fifteen beliefs and identify boundaries for each. Think about and write down different real-life situations and how far things can go before your family boundaries will be violated. Having too many boundaries can confuse the whole family and make it impossible to grow and adapt.

After you choose the top ten to fifteen boundaries, talk out some rules to keep them from being violated. You cannot set down rules within your family without your teenager understanding the basic beliefs behind the rules, or without defining specific boundaries and consequences. Arbitrariness will simply add to the chaos and confuse your teens. It is simply asking for trouble and growing frustration. Allowing your teen to face the natural consequences for breaking the rules is the number one way to help him learn how to honor your beliefs. Deciding on the rules should be a family job. Your teens might surprise you with their thoughts on where there should be rules. Where you thought your teen was not struggling, you may come to find that he or she really needs a defined boundary and rule in that area of life.

Most of us work for companies that have a policy manual. We follow the policies, since they are a requirement for enjoying the financial benefits and privileges of employment. From the policies, we know what to expect, how to act, and how not to act if we want to keep our jobs. Likewise, the rules within your family Belief System will help each family member know what is expected, how to act, where the lines are drawn between right and wrong behavior, and the consequences for stepping over the line.

How Do We Set Fair Rules and Deliver Appropriate Consequences?

"We're lost on this whole concept of developing rules and following through on consequences. Our son tells us he doesn't have to listen to anything we say, and he's going to do what he wants. In addition, whenever he does get in trouble, we have a hard time following through on any consequences. It's like we live in a world that is being governed by our sixteen year-old son. It's gotten to the point that I think my wife is going to leave me if I don't make something different happen in our home. Thoughts?"

Rules are expectations and guidelines placed around our behavior, in order to support our family boundaries and Belief System. So, how do we go about creating and implementing rules that will effectively guide teens for their own good, and for the good of the entire family?

Rules for your home will most likely fall into three main areas of concern that are foundational to all other character issues. These are honesty, obedience, and respect. Rules should be relevant, attainable and beneficial, not a source of shame, frustration, or failure. After all, isn't the ultimate intent to keep a child's poor choices from consuming him and destroying his relationships with others?

Therefore, when you think about the rules that govern your home, you might want to ask yourself two questions: *"How much will this rule matter after I am gone?"* and *"Will this help build my child's character and cause him to become more mature or responsible?"* If the answer to either question is "no," then you probably need to rethink the rule and your motivation for wanting to make it a rule. Rules also need to make sense. We can all think about rules set down by our own parents that made no sense at all, and we can recall others that were beneficial to us (even though we may not have liked them).

Finally, rules often need to evolve over time, as lessons are learned, and kept in line with the growing maturity of your teenager. Out of date, irrelevant or demeaning rules will lead to animosity, loss of respect and rebellion. They can also lead to consequence confusion, since outdated rules are often not enforced. Regularly update your rules and restate them to your teenagers, awarding them with freedom and added privileges for the progress they make.

For teenagers, the loss of a privilege can be a powerful consequence. Sometimes they don't realize how many privileges they enjoy—at least, not until they lose them for a time.

Thinking about rules brings to mind a time when we had several teenage boys living with us in our own home years ago. Based on the worsening condition of their bathroom, I could see that they needed help with exercising more self-control. I told them, "Guys, from now on, you need to clean your own toilet and keep your bathroom clean. If not, you could lose it." Unfortunately, they ignored the rule and the mess got even worse. The once pearly white toilet bowl turned some not-so-lovely shades of brown. So, one day, I just took the entire toilet out. I literally removed it from the house. By that time, the toilet needed to be replaced anyway, so I thought not having it for awhile would be a good learning opportunity for them.

When they got home from school, there was nothing but a little hole in the floor where the brown toilet used to stand. They said, "Where are we supposed to go?" I said, "Aim well. I'm sorry, the rule is that you need to clean your toilet and keep your bathroom clean. If you won't clean it, you can't have it." After a few days of not aiming all that well and the stench becoming unbearable, they came to me and asked, "What do we need to do to get our toilet back?"

I said, "Well, I appreciate you coming back and asking. The thing is...you can have your toilet back, but to make sure you have learned this lesson, you also have to clean the toilets in the whole house for the next couple of months." They readily agreed, and I installed a new toilet. They cleaned all the bathrooms for a few months and learned the importance of taking better care of things. The most important lesson for them was that when you break a rule, you pay the consequences.

The consequence in my example may sound crude, but it got the point across. After that, they kept the bathroom clean, and they listened more carefully when I announced other important rules.

Setting up rules and enforcing consequences—more than any other thing you manage as a parent—is the best way to help your child learn right from wrong and to change from selfish to unselfish thinking.

When you create rules, make it clear that they are developed in the context of longing for your child to do well in life, more than from a selfish need for you to be in control. Rules are not just about having your house operate well and getting the chores done. In the toilet example I gave, I saw it as a major opportunity to teach these boys an important life principle about responsibility - not just make that side of our house smell better. It is a lesson they still recall today.

Above all, keep in mind that your relationship with your children is more important than any rule. Don't tie rule keeping or rule breaking to your love or acceptance of them. Let them know that you will continue to love them, even when they mess up. Continually say the phrase that should be very familiar to you by now, *"There is nothing you can do to make me love you more, and nothing you can do to make me love you less."*

Some parents confuse the idea of rule making with ruling their home. Reasonable rule making and proper boundaries will help a teenager mature into a confident adult, while living under a "ruler" can lead to frustration, rebellion and eroded self-esteem. Which kind of home is yours? One that has rules, or one that is ruled?

"Ruling" works and is necessary when kids are younger, but as your children reach the teenage years, they naturally begin weighing decisions on their own. When they choose to break the household rules, they need to deal with the resulting consequences. Teenagers understand consequences. That's how they learn, not from lecturing or parental anger.

When teenagers butt heads with a "ruler," conflict and frustration will result. The only thing they'll learn is either how to better hide their improper actions or how to scream louder than the ruler does. Neither of these is productive and can also lead to a legacy of poor parenting when they have their own families.

Rules need to be communicated in advance, right along with the consequences for breaking those rules. Think of it this way: If no one knows the rules, then your teenager will have to learn them by trial and error and will constantly get into trouble. Likewise, if consequences for breaking the rules aren't known, then a teenager has no way to weigh those consequences against whatever pleasure he may find in breaking the rule. This balancing of actions versus consequences is a critical skill for adolescents to learn and exercise.

Finally, rules need to evolve as lessons are learned, keeping in line with the growing maturity of your teenager. I'm not talking about "giving in." I'm saying once again that out-of-date, irrelevant or demeaning rules will lead to animosity, loss of respect and rebellion by your teenager. Remember, "ruling" your home is not a good measurement of the effectiveness of your rule making.

Consequences

If I asked, "Does your teen seem sensible?" Most parents would look at me cross-eyed or ask me if I've lost my mind. "Of course, my teen isn't sensible!" Teens are wired for chaos, and they spread it everywhere they go, including your home. Our job as parents is to help our teenagers become sensible, as well as responsible and mature. The best way to help our teens move in that direction is to allow consequences to teach them when they make bad choices.

Consequences for teenagers should never hurt physically (other than aching muscles from work assignments). They should never be demeaning or undermine the child's self-esteem. For teenagers, the loss of a privilege is the most reasonable and powerful consequence. Think about some reasonable consequences for your home, and keep in mind how important it is that they are communicated well in advance so the teenager doesn't attribute the consequences they receive to your poor mood or a bad day. When they break a rule, they should know exactly what the consequence will be. And just like laws in our society, parents need to build in progressively stronger consequences for rules that are broken again and again (since the initial consequence was obviously not enough of a deterrent).

Don't correlate your teen's rule keeping or rule breaking to your love or acceptance of him. Express your sorrow when your teen experiences consequences, but take care not to express your disappointment in him. There's a big difference between those two sentiments. One is caring, and the other is destructive of your relationship.

The Parent's Admonition: *"There is nothing you can do to make me love you more, and nothing you can do to make me love you less."*

When your teenagers break a rule (and they will), show your deep love for them by refusing to let them off the hook. Teenagers mostly learn from consequences. So avoid taking the consequences away or lessening them. When consequences are known well in advance, it shouldn't damage your relationship when they are handed out. Surely, your teenager weighed the consequences at the moment they chose to step over the line, and they chose to do it anyway!

Lay out some rules for your home, and begin to think about what consequences to apply. Decide things like the following: who pays for what, what timeframe is expected for certain things like curfew and chores, what you expect from your child in terms of school behavior and grades, work, their spiritual life, their friends. Address issues like respect, honesty and obedience with clear rules—no lying, no cheating, and everyone gets respect. Examine how your rules support your boundaries and beliefs for the way your home should run. Call a family meeting and work on the rules and consequences together, so everyone is part of it. You'll be surprised. Your teen will often suggest penalizing bad behavior with consequences more severe than you were thinking.

Teenagers won't learn just from parental warnings. Most of us have tried that without much success. And unfortunately, one or both parents all too often cave in. We step in to lessen the consequences when our teen gets in trouble. Each time we do so, a valuable lesson is not learned and a mistake is apt to be repeated.

The point is this: Teens learn best by making mistakes and suffering a bit from the consequences. They remember the lessons when there are consequences because they are then able to figure out for themselves if the punishment was worth the pain.

Recently, we were with some of the kids from *Heartlight*, having a blast in the woods, annihilating one another with paintballs. The kids especially loved plastering me. When we finished, I was surprised to see that one of the boys refused to clean his paintball equipment.

I said to him, "You played paintball. We had a good time, and you know the rule for the course—everybody cleans their own equipment."

"Well, I am not going to do it," he said, and then unleashed a verbal tirade.

I remained calm and said to him, "Now we have another problem. In addition to breaking the equipment cleaning rule, you are also being disrespectful to me." I laid down consequences for his disrespect and his refusal to cooperate. He would be required to do a specified amount of yard work and lose his extra privileges for a time. And he would still have to clean the paintball equipment and apologize for mouthing off.

After a couple of days raking pine needles, he came to me to apologize. As I got the equipment out for him to clean, I brought the lesson home and reaffirmed him saying, "You are a good man, but you need to work through the way you respond when you are angry. It is killing your relationships. Your friends and others will not put up with it. I want something better for you. By the way, this lesson is not about cleaning the stupid paintball stuff. This is about helping you be successful in life."

Because of the consequences, he already knew that. Time and work had allowed him to figure out a very important lesson, not just about being responsible for things, but also about being responsible for his own behavior.

Give Them Something That Can Be Taken Away.

You may ask me, "How do I know what kind of consequence to apply?" I tell parents that one way is to give them something they want, but teach them they could lose it if they don't follow the rules. When they don't follow the rules, take it away for a time.

When thinking about consequences, it helps to know what your children value. If they don't value it, they won't learn from losing it. Is it time with friends, text messaging, car privileges, the cell phone, music, the computer, or after-school events? Also, make sure the consequence relates to the privilege. A simple example might be, "If the car isn't home by curfew tonight, then you won't be able to use the car tomorrow." If he continues to miss curfew each time he is given car privileges, then don't let him drive for increasingly longer periods. Don't even offer rides to school. Let him take the bus, so he learns from it.

Most of all, keep it calm. Keep your anger and that "I'm-disappointed-in-you" statement out of it altogether. Take the opposite approach and side with your teen in how sad you feel that they have to experience the consequence. Our goal with consequences is to make the teen angry at himself or herself for knowingly doing something stupid, not to make your teen deflect the anger onto you for being a "jerk" about it!

If you haven't done such a good job of communicating rules and consequences up until this point, then start now. Let your teen know you've blown it when it comes to certain areas of discipline, and you will be making a change that affects everyone soon. Give kids time to adjust to the idea that discipline is going to be different before you let them know exactly how it will look.

After you have allowed them a little time to get used to the idea, call everyone together and work out your ideas for rules and consequences together. When it comes time to give a consequence, your teens will already understand exactly what to expect and exactly why to expect it. In fact, they will tell you what their consequence is, because they weighed it in their minds and deliberately chose to accept it when they broke the rule. *Working* out consequences well ahead of time helps everyone remain calm when your teens experience the consequences related to breaking the rules.

Some parents are surprised by the concept of "managing consequences." They manage their budget. They manage their calendar. They may even manage employees. But most have never heard of managing consequences. Still, I can't emphasize it enough. This is one of the most vital things you'll do in parenting adolescents. If you want your teenager to become responsible and mature, you have to let them take responsibility for their actions and feel the sting of consequences.

Let Your Teen Feel the Full Force of Being Caught If He Commits Illegal Acts.

Illegal behavior calls for consequences that get your teen's undivided attention. Such consequences are often out of your control anyway, but they shouldn't be lessened in any way by you. I've known some parents who are quite justified in their desire for their drug-abusing teenager to be caught by the police before they sink even deeper into that lifestyle. Refusing to bail a teenager out of jail or delaying that action a day or two is another example of allowing natural consequences to take their course. An appearance all alone before a judge and being processed into jail have a way of catching a teen's attention and changing behavior like nothing else can. A key point is to let your teens know in advance that you won't bail them out if they are at fault.

There are two sides to consequences—the tough side that says to your teen, "I will allow painful consequences to take place in order to teach you when you do something wrong," and the tender side which says, "I will always love you no matter what you do, and it truly hurts me to allow consequences in your life."

Your teen needs and wants a taste of the character of God. Teens want to experience the strength of a warrior and the tender, caring side of somebody promising to help them get through their difficulties. So, even if you are dealing with painful consequences, make sure your teens know you love them, no matter what they've done.

Consequences, when applied correctly or allowed to happen naturally, change your child's thinking. They teach adolescents how to think or act differently the next time.

Practice makes perfect. For example, when we hear a child practice music lessons, she makes mistakes, practices more, and makes some more mistakes. Eventually, with enough practice, she gets it right, and we jump for joy. The same is true for decision-making. With enough practice, your child can learn to become a good decision-maker, and to become mature, responsible, and trustworthy.

Handing over some control and setting good boundaries is essential to fostering maturity in your teen. However, we parents often don't realize that unless we allow our child to take full responsibility for their behavior by facing consequences, our teenager will remain immature. I deal with this constantly in my work with struggling teens and their parents, who wonder why their teen is so out of control.

At the heart of this issue is one central theme - consequences. If you wonder why teenagers behave irresponsibly, well, it's because they *are* irresponsible. And they will not become responsible, mature, or wise until they engage in the process of dealing with the consequences of their choices and behavior. It is a cycle that needs to happen over and over before a teen comes to full maturity.

Sometimes a parent says, "Wouldn't it be best to wait until I trust my child before I give him more responsibility or control, so he won't have such difficult consequences?" My answer is that if you wait until you trust teens, you will never give them any responsibility. You never will, and they won't learn how to face consequences and learn from them, or the consequences they face later on will be of a much more serious nature.

Don't Wait. Start Early!

Building responsibility and good decision-making takes practice, and you have to start earlier than you think. It is a learned process. As the writer of Hebrews says,

> *"But solid food is for the mature, who by constant use have trained themselves to distinguish good from evil..."*
> (Hebrews 5:14, NIV)

Did you notice the words "constant use"? That means again and again and again. So start giving responsibilities early. Teach them in sixth grade how to balance a checkbook. Give them a debit card with their allowance on it so they learn early how to manage it. Get an alarm clock, and let them wake themselves up for school every morning. Let them keep a calendar or planner and be responsible for letting you know in advance when they need transportation to and from events. If they forget to discuss it in advance, they miss the activity or event. The consequence of not communicating about the calendar is, "You don't get to go."

When they begin driving, agree to periodically put money on a gas card. Then, when they prematurely run out of their gas allowance, don't give them more. I guarantee it will be the last time they run out. In the process, they will figure out how to manage their gas money.

The idea here is to stop helping your teenagers so much, the way you helped them when they were younger. While a major responsibility of good parenting is certainly to control and protect our children, parents must make room for their older children to make mistakes. You help a teen best by letting him deal with the natural results of decisions, fall down a bit in the process, and figure out how to get back up.

In many cases, parents take control because they see the absence of a child's self-control, and there is a display of immaturity and irresponsibility. Parents of struggling teens often feel forced into the mode of over-control. Over-control happens when otherwise loving parents protect their children from the consequences of their mistakes, or when they set too-strict rules and limits (Example: Not wanting them to be with other peers for fear that they will learn bad habits, get hurt, etc.). Over-controlled children are more likely to have problems with peer dependence, relationship enmeshment conflicts and difficulty setting and keeping firm boundaries. They may also have problems taking risks and being creative. Every culture on earth has a proverb that resembles this one: *If you rescue them once, you will just have to rescue them again.*

Handing teenagers control and allowing them to face the consequences of their own decisions means:

- They may get an "F" on their homework when they don't turn in the homework. When they get enough F's, they will flunk the class. If they flunk the class, they will have to make it up in summer school. If they don't make it up in summer school, they won't graduate. (Believe me, I've seen it happen just this way.)
- They may have to walk to school, pay for a cab, or miss an entire day when they don't get up in time to make the bus. If they miss school, they miss the fun after school or that weekend as well. After the first time (when you may choose to administer grace), don't write the excuse that gets them out of the consequences.
- If they serve detention at school, then let them miss the football game on Friday night as well.
- If they use the Internet to promote an inappropriate image or lifestyle, disconnect it for a period of time.
- If they get arrested, and it is obvious that they or the friends they were hanging around with are at fault, let them sit in jail for awhile. Don't bail them out right away. Sitting in jail can have a sobering affect and force them to reevaluate their life's direction.
- If they are ticketed for speeding, not wearing their seat belt, being out past the local curfew, or other infractions of the law, let them figure out how to pay the fine, as well as how to get to work or school the next day, since they will not be driving your car.
- Let them help pay for their insurance and gas when they are ready to start driving. Don't even get their license until they can pay their portion of the first quarter of insurance.
- Pay for college as long as they maintain their grades at a level you both agree is appropriate. If grades become unsatisfactory, then let them pay for the next semester. If you are paying for college, tell them which schools you are willing to pay for. If they wish to attend elsewhere, they can pay for it.
- If they spend their money foolishly, don't buy the things they need. Let them figure out how to pay for those things

(like extra gas money). Doing without may teach them to stop spending foolishly.

- If they are experimenting with drugs or alcohol, require them to pass periodic and unannounced drug and alcohol tests as a requirement to live in your house.
- Let them decide how to pay for college *next* semester if they spent this semester partying rather than studying. Don't finance an apartment or a car if they continue with that lifestyle. Let them decide how to finance that lifestyle themselves.
- Turn off the TV, remove the TV, or cancel your cable if they continue to view inappropriate content. Loss of the TV is an appropriate consequence.

You are not being a bad parent by allowing these consequences to happen. Letting them experience consequences for poor reasoning is the *best* thing you can do for teenagers.

Pre-teens are just a few short years away from driving, earning, and spending. Make it your goal to create the environment early-on where they learn responsibility and grow into maturity. You want them to experience the fruit of the Spirit, which is self-control. You want them to make good decisions and not be controlled by unhealthy things.

Are you willing to begin to relinquish control and help your teenager find out who he is and who God desires for him to be? It doesn't mean you stop helping your child. It means that you wait to be invited into the problem-solving process, and you don't solve problems for him. You let him face the music and experience the consequences of his own decisions. You set new boundaries, and let him move in the direction he decides works best for him.

You may have to repeat this process several times before your teen gets it right, so hang in there. Eventually your teen will get it, learn how to make good decisions, and avoid unwanted consequences.

How Can We Be Consistent When We're "Part-Time" Parents?

"How do you handle behavioral issues when a teen lives in two homes, and the other parent does not have boundaries, rules, or direct consequences for inappropriate behavior? In fact, the other parent allows our child to participate in activities that we've told him he can't do, and the other parent encourages it! How do we address these difficulties? We catch him lying, acting inappropriately, and violating our standards and principles because his mother feels otherwise. What do we do?"

If you are divorced and your teen moves between two households with two different sets of standards, you don't need me to tell you that there is a lot of room for manipulation of the boundaries. And you need to face the fact, if you haven't already, that you can't control the other household.

What I'm going to tell you at the very beginning of my comments is to stick with the rules, boundaries, and consequences that you believe to be right for your home. That's the best you can do—be consistent with what you believe.

There's no use complicating the effects of divorce by causing more problems in the life of your child. Teens want and need rules, curfews, restrictions, boundaries, directives, marching orders, challenges, and people placed before them to insure that they are walking a path that will keep them headed in the right direction and prevent them from ending up in a place where they don't want to be.

Of course, the best-case scenario for teens is when their parents, the ex-spouses, work hard to have an amicable relationship. Co-parenting means communication lines are established, and there is agreement about what is allowed and what is not allowed in both homes in regards to the rearing of your teen.

However, my observations tell me that this is not usually the case. My observations also tell me that there are just some things that aren't going to change, and the acceptance of what cannot be changed is far less stressful than beating your head against a wall trying to get someone else to change.

I believe there are several reasons why there is such a wide variation in the rules between former spouses. These may include proving or justifying why they are not together (*"See how different we are?"* They may ask the kids.), revenge on the former spouse, or guilt over the fact that the divorce caused their children pain and they don't want to add to it by inflicting punishment. Some divorced parents don't want to enforce rules and consequences because they're just tired of conflict. Any of these reasons should not be an excuse for allowing teens to unleash bad behavior on either household without consequences. It just doesn't bear good fruit in the lives of the kids and will cost them much more in the long run.

An understanding of the motivation behind the differences, however, can help you understand why your child has a hard time conforming to your boundaries and can help your child understand why the rules in your home will be applied and enforced, regardless of what happens in the other home. You're not going to change anything in the life of your ex. Try as you may, you've got to control only that which you can control and allow your former spouse to control what they have control over.

Hold to what you believe to be right for your teen, and uphold the standards that you want for them. Your teen is capable of living in two different places under two sets of rules. They do it all the time. There are rules at school that are different than rules at work. Rules are different at an airport than they are at a hospital. Teens are flexible and resilient. They can adapt to what is required.

What they will want to do is manipulate to get what they want. It is the nature of teens to do so, and if parents don't eliminate the possibility of this manipulation, it will continue. Your rules, expectations, and boundaries can help a teen learn this flexibility and develop a great sense of respect for you, especially if it's been lost because of something you did wrong in the marriage to cause the divorce (or something your child believes you did). Respect can be regained.

Your teen may choose to go live at their mother or father's home to get out of your rules and expectations. If that's the case, ask those around you if you are being too strict. Maybe it isn't a case of your ex having no rules, but an imbalance because you have so many. Or maybe your ex has relaxed the rules to counteract the impression she has (right or wrong) that you have handed out too many. Try to make your rules reasonable, so that this is not the motive behind your ex's actions and the driving force behind your teen's desire to spend more time elsewhere.

If older teens choose to move in to the "rule-less" home, and there's nothing you can do about it, you can still support them without changing your stance on what is allowed in your home. And you can still not like their choices. The rejection of what you desire for your child isn't always a rejection of the relationship. So don't give up the relationship out of your hurt feelings because your child decides to move elsewhere. This is the perfect time to practice what you preach: *"Nothing you do could make me love you any less..."* Teens have to make some choices in their lives, and some of the best lessons are learned when they experience the results and effects of those choices.

What I have seen over the long haul for teens who have parents at the opposite ends of the rules and expectation spectrum is that, early in their teen years, kids want freedom and will fight for independence whether parents are divorced or not. In later adolescent years, they long for someone to think of them first, want the best for them, and design a path that helps them achieve their goals. That path includes rules, consequences, freedom to make choices, and boundaries. When a teen "catches" the vision and intent of a parent's actions, he eventually moves toward that parent.

Let me ask you a question: Would you rather have a "happy" teen now with no rules and expectations, or a teen who matures and has a healthy relationship with you—and others— in their later years...when she is married, has kids, and desires the security of a parent who thinks in her best interest? Easy answer, but sometimes a hard process.

Hang in there. The short-term trials of dealing with an uncooperative "ex" will one day be over. Once your child finishes schooling, turns eighteen, or moves out, you won't have to contend with the inconsistencies, lack of support, or the ranting about how tough or strict you are. Don't give up just because it gets hard. It's called loving your teen, even if she doesn't always like you.

QUESTION 28

How Do We Motivate an Underachiever?

"Our son is doing just enough to get by and seems to have lost any desire to do well in school, at our home, within the church, or with his friends. It's almost as if he's given up. How do we motivate him to better things?"

There are a number of sides to this answer.

The Easy Answer

One side of the answer is that this teen might be bordering on depression and needs some help getting through some tough times. Whenever parents see a rapid change in their teen's behavior, a "red flag" should go up that merely says, *"Something's changing here, and I don't want to miss anything."* Any time a parent sees a big behavioral, academic, or relational change, there should be alarm and possible action.

I also believe that you can get anyone to do just about anything with the right motivation. It would cause me to wonder why a teen has lost a desire to do well. A young man doesn't have much more than school, home, church, and friends; and it sounds like he's "thrown in the towel" on all of them for some reason.

First, I would wonder if something has happened in his social circle. Has he been rejected, hurt, disappointed, cast out, or ridiculed? Pinpointing particular actions by friends or a girlfriend allow for an easier discussion than just stating that you want a teen ₒo well." I would definitely dig a little deeper with questions, ₒscussions, time together, and a sharing of hearts. Just as all of a teen's behavior is goal-oriented in pursuit of getting what they want, their non-behavior is just as goal-oriented in preventing what they don't want.

The Harder Answer

The other side of this answer for me would be to ask another question, "*What are the* better things *that you're talking about*? Sometimes a child sees the futility of his efforts and says, "*I'm done, I can't do it anymore; I am flat worn out.*" The world today is a tough place to grow up, and too often, well-meaning parents place expectations on a child that make living even harder, not easier.

I swam competitively for thirteen years. I remember one year during our off-season, my three-hundred-pound swim coach asked that we participate in "track" as well. For some odd reason, he thought that I'd be able to do the high jump. I knew from the beginning that his choice for me was wrong, as I had a six-inch vertical jump and possessed the tiniest little chicken legs that were great for swimming but not a good resource for the high jump.

At track practice, we'd always begin the workouts by running a few laps around the stadium. They were just enough to wear out my little legs that were supposed to then catapult me to victory as I sailed through the air over a horizontal pole that, I swear, seemed to be eight feet in the air.

I recall him showing me in slow motion how to perfect the art of the high jump. He called it the "Fosbury Flop." I called it "Mission Impossible." I laughed then, watching him coach me to do something that he'd never be able to do. And I still chuckle over the images in my memory of him when I see Shamu leaping out of the water at Sea World.

I knew that the chances of me getting over that pole were slim to none, and that he could have me jump, practice, and work my tail off until I was blue in the face; but my body was not going to make it over that eight-foot mark. As I would run toward the high jump bar during practice, I kept reciting, "I think I can, I think I can..." and picturing myself as a little engine that could.

It didn't work.

I remember going to him and telling him that I just didn't think I would be able to compete in this event. His answer? He handed me a jump rope and said I needed to go home and strengthen my legs. I quit the next day.

What was the problem? The bar was too high. I figured that out on my own. That bar, for me, represented failure, defeat, frustration, pain, and humiliation. When I quit, I felt the greatest relief of my high school life. For a number of reasons, I look back on that time I quit and feel like it was one of the best decisions of my high school years.

My coach told me that I had lost my drive. In so many words, he said that I was a quitter and a loser. He assured me that if I didn't master the high jump, I would not be able to make it as a swimmer in my later years. He shamed me. He tried to make me feel guilty. What he thought he was doing right in trying to motivate me only discouraged me. It also got in between our relationship. For you see, he really wasn't thinking of me; he was thinking more about his need to have a high jumper.

Eventually, I proved the coach wrong about being a quitter and a loser, as I received a full-ride athletic scholarship to the University of Arkansas upon my high school graduation. In swimming, not track.

There are times when parents set the bar way too high for their teens, resulting in nothing but frustration and the eventual damaging of a once-healthy relationship. This is a part of the harder answer. Maybe the bar that you are setting for your teen is seen by your teen as too high, fruitless or frivolous. Perhaps what you see as a loss of desire is really a healthy response to an unattainable expectation.

Things to Carefully Consider

If you want to evaluate whether your teen is lazy, or if you have set the bar of expectations too high, ask yourself some of the following questions:

Is it really important to you for your child to make all A's on her report card? What if your child isn't an "A" student? What if your teen is really just a "C" student? I tell the young people who live with us at Heartlight to attend class and do the work that's being asked of them. That's all we require. This does two things. My statement transfers responsibility for their grades to them so that they learn to study, to do what is required, and "buy into" their education. The second thing my statement accomplishes is that it lets them know that my relationship with them isn't about good grades or bad grades.

I want them to be educated, but it's not my highest priority for them. I would suggest that there are much more important bars to leap over than just the academic bar.

Some of those include learning to become a good friend, becoming a servant, living with humility, enduring hardship and tough times, loving God and walking under His guidance, and touching the hearts of others. Are these "bars"? Sure! And in my book, they're all much more important than academics. Think about it. At your workplace, do you want to sit in a cubicle every day next to the guy who was the top of his class and struts like he knows it or next to the empathetic coworker who genuinely wants to know how your wife and kids are doing?

So ask yourself where you are pushing. Do you push your children in athletics? Do you push them into activities that they only participate in because they feel like you'd be disappointed if they didn't? Do you tell your child (in so many ways) that you want her to be perfect? Why do your children need to look a certain way? Do you give them permission not to have it all together? Has church for them become a "filling station" or a "draining station"? Do they feel like their success is a reflection of your success as a parent?

If you are ready to find out the truth, ask your kids. Your discussion with them might keep them from shutting down and bailing out. The conversation might just relieve your children of self-inflicted misinterpretation of what you want *for* them and help them understand your motives when you want something *from* them.

QUESTION

What If Our Prodigal Won't Get Out?

"Our son doesn't follow our rules, won't listen to us when we give direction, ignores our conversations, is angry all the time, and treats his younger brothers and sisters terribly. It's almost as if he's a stranger in our home. We have told him that if he can't abide by our rules and respect his family members, he cannot live in our home. He refuses to leave. Any advice?"

Let me share a little story. After a long week recently, what I thought would be just a quick jaunt to the local Best Buy electronics store to pick up the new Alison Krauss and Robert Plant CD (a work designed to appeal to my love for bluegrass and passion for Led Zeppelin mixed together) turned into an observation platform from which to view the more immature side of adolescence and early adulthood. My intention was just to walk in and walk out. What lured me to stay was the snapshot of immaturity I saw, and continued to see, as I watched three different young men of about fifteen to twenty-seven years old (or so). Here's what I observed:

People were gathered around the guy who had to be in his midtwenties to watch this tall, lanky fellow play the newest version of "Guitar Hero," an interactive video game where the player coordinates the pressing of five buttons and strumming of a handheld guitar to the visual and audio prompts on a video screen. The goal is to correctly play along with the cues on the screen. It's a fun game, but people shouldn't take themselves too seriously or think that they can actually play the guitar because they can play the game. This young man did both. And boy, did he put on a show.

He danced as he played, jumping in the air, bellowing out, "Oh, Yeah!" every time that he nailed the harder chord progressions. I thought that the others around him were his friends. They weren't. None of us standing there knew him. No one except one other person. His mother.

I thought he was joking around entertaining us. When I realized he wasn't joking, I became a little embarrassed that I was sitting there watching him, feeling like I was either laughing at a retarded person, or somehow applauding someone who was obviously living out a fantasy of not having to grow up. This guy was serious. He really thought that he knew how to play a guitar and was so proud of himself for his Guitar Hero accomplishments.

The point is that what was funny at first glance was really a little bit tragic. If this young man was thirteen or fourteen, that would have been one thing. But that wasn't the case. As I stood next to his mother, I commented in jest, "He's good." Her comment back to me? "This is the only thing he's done since he graduated from college. He's had a hard time finding a job...I wish he could get paid for playing video games."

I walked away thinking, "Well, that's different." I thought back to when I was twenty-seven. I had been married six years, had two kids, and was working my tail off to make a living. The "old man" in me thought about where I was now. Watching a twenty-seven-year-old "boy" at five o'clock in the afternoon stuck in a world of immaturity.

I continued to look for my CD and, upon walking back to the shrinking CD music section of the store, found a nineteen-year-old playing a war video game with a six-year-old kid. This nineteen-year-old was cussing, doing the "Oh yeah!" thing (although he wasn't related to the twenty-seven-year-old), acting like a complete goof. He looked scraggly, unkempt, and unshaven, with pants halfway down his butt and a tattoo of a skull and crossbones peeking out of his long shorts. On the other leg was a caricature of the cartoon dog Scooby Doo with a caption that read "F--- the government." This nineteen-year-old "boy" was totally clueless about how loud he was, the offensive verbiage he used, and how childish he really looked.

For a moment, I really thought that a "short bus" had pulled up outside Best Buy and some group had brought "the kids" out for field trip. I couldn't believe it. Then this guy's girlfriend walked up to him, patted him on his exposed rear end, and said, "Come on, I found the game."

I found my CD and discovered the one bright spot of my excursion to this store—I looked at Robert Plant's picture and felt young.

As I got in line to check out, there was a young man of about fifteen demanding that his mother buy the latest computer game system and throwing a childish fit when she said, "We'll have to talk to your Dad." The young man was relentless. His language was foul and disrespectful. He was demanding everything. The mother looked scared. She was embarrassed. I was, too, as was the young check-out lady. This young man treated his mother like dirt. He acted rude and arrogant, and his behavior was childish and immature. I thought to myself, "If I'd said anything like that or treated my mother like that, my dad would have knocked me halfway into next week."

I looked at the young man, and our eyes caught. He didn't even care that he was throwing a "fit." He probably had no idea that he was. What I thought to be abnormal was really normal for this young punk. His display of disrespect and "demanding-ness" (Is that a word? Because if it isn't, it's an accurate description of this young man's behavior and attitude.) was tragic at best.

It angered me. I felt no sense of sorrow. I felt anger, and I don't think it was just because my trip to pick up some soothing music was tainted by my exposure to this "Tragic Trio." I was angered because I really felt that the world I walked into that afternoon and the world in which I was raised were two entirely different places. As I walked to my car, I wondered to myself about this generation—the one that my generation has created.

Now I am not saying that all kids who frequent electronic stores are immature nerds who don't want to grow up. Please don't limit my comments to these retail venues nor apply them to think that

I'm saying everyone acts this way. But you know it when you see it. And it's especially concerning when it is your child.

I see it everywhere. I hear it from parents everyday. There are too many immature "kids" (past the age of eighteen) who won't grow up, who are unprepared and who act as if everyone owes them everything, without them having to work for it.

And it's not just the guys. There may be more public activities that guys can be involved in that display their immaturity in front of others, but I see the same lack of maturity in many girls.

I was at a mall in southern California a few weeks ago when I witnessed a young (maybe fourteen-year-old) girl following her mother, begging and pleading that she be allowed to go back to the store and get the purse she wanted. The mother, in her frustration, was walking away, not saying a word, displaying in her silence a confusion over not knowing what to do amidst embarrassment over watching her fourteen-year-old act like a six-year-old. This young lady acted as if she was "owed" that purse, and her goal was to demand long and loudly until she got her way.

My years have taught me that if you push long enough, something's gotta give. She pushed, and her mother gave in. Her mother gave in because she didn't know what to do—not because she wanted to buy her daughter the purse, but because she wanted the feeling of discomfort over how her daughter was acting to end. She wanted it go away. And it did. When the daughter had the purse in hand, Mom got the daughter off her back. And the lesson learned by the daughter was that her immature tactic worked. Guess what she'll do the next time she wants something?

I think all these kids I have mentioned are prodigals. They may still live at home, but they are prodigal in their behavior. Prodigal is defined by phrases like "to drive away", to "squander," or by "profuse or wasteful expenditure." Another definition is a "reckless spendthrift." One Internet dictionary says the noun prodigal means, "One who spends or gives foolishly."[1]

Immature teens—prodigals—want it. They want it now. They want to do as they please. They don't want anyone telling them what to do. They live in foolishness. And they'll squander everything they have.

That sounds like the prodigal in Scripture, doesn't it? Except today's prodigal doesn't want to leave home. He's too comfortable. So he stays, acting like a prodigal, and never comes to his senses, as was the fulfillment (and hope) of the story in the book of Luke. They stay because parents allow it, feed it, and don't know what to do to stop it.

I always encourage parents to come up with a plan to move this child into adulthood by transitioning them into maturity through a working together of requirements, limits, decreasing support, and enticements to provide a plan to help a young person grow up. After your graduated teen has completed his or her vacation from the rigors of high school, a conversation must happen that communicates that you would desire for your teen to take some steps toward adulthood. Let me give you some examples for each area mentioned of what I would say to a child who might be more content with doing nothing than something. The goal is to move them from just sitting around at home doing nothing and still dependent on parents to moving them to do those things needed for independence.

Requirements

- If you're going to live at home, you're going to have to be working full time.
- We will review every month whether our arrangement at home is "working" and have a discussion about any needed changes.
- Alcohol, drugs, or tobacco, are not allowed in our home.
- You are to do your own laundry, mow the yard once a week, and take care of your dog,
- There will be no disrespect, deceitfulness, or dishonesty.
- You can't bring people that we don't know into the house unless we are present and have given our permission.
- We don't run an apartment house and will continue to eat meals as a family. You can participate if you want.

Limits

- We won't charge you rent, but we will expect you to take care of that which you have been given.

- The curfew at our home remains at 12:00 midnight. You can come and go as you please within that time frame.
- You'll have to pay for your own gas and spending money. There's no weekly allowance.
- You will have to pay for all your clothes, dates, and purchases. You will not have to pay for food that you eat.
- If you get arrested, we will not post bail.
- When parents are out of town, there are to be not guests or parties at the house.
- You cannot be a negative influence on your siblings, nor be counter-productive to what we desire for their life. Our limits on videos, music, and morals remain unchanged and we expect your support by your actions and comments within our home.

Decreasing Support
- In 6 months, after you've settled into a job, you'll have to move into an apartment. We'll pay 100% of the first 2 months rent, 75% of the next two months rent, 50% of the following 2 months, 25% of the next two months. After 8 months of my support, you'll have to pay your own rent.
- We'll pay for your car insurance on the same time table.

Enticements
- Should you maintain your job for 6 months, I'll give you a $200 bonus.
- Don't get any speeding tickets for a year, and I'll buy you a new set of tires.
- Get a DUI and I won't cut off any body parts; I'll just take back the tires.

Someone might read the list that I've listed above and say, "Mark, you haven't limited any of the video game playing, bar hopping, or the hangin' out time." You're absolutely right! What I have found is that as parents formulate requirements and communicates financial parameters that must be met by their teen, these extra-periphery past-times (like video games) usually pass.

My encouragement to parents is to not let your home become an escape from the world or a hindrance to a teen's normal maturation process. I call that "subsidized immaturity." By not requiring something of your teen to help him or her grow up, you are helping them remain a child full of childish thinking. I haven't met a parent who desires for their young twenty-five -year-old to have a mindset and lifestyle of an eighteen-year-old. But I have met many parents that have kids that fit that description because they have indeed provided, and thus enabled, their child to remain in the childish and foolish mindset. Remaining in that childish and foolish mindset can best be described throughout the book of Proverbs in all the verses that describe a "fool." Take a marker and highlight all those Scriptures in Proverbs that mention the word "fool", and you'll see the need for parents to take a stand and help their teen mature. It doesn't take much reading in the book of Proverbs to see that the "way of the fool" leads to future destruction.

How Do I Help My Hurting Teen When He Is Hurting Others?

"My son is so mean to us (his parents) and his brothers and sisters. He's vile in his words, and his actions express nothing but contempt for anyone else around him. His attitude is sour, and his discussions are always an argument. It's almost as if he hurts people as a payback for what has happened in his life. Could this be the result of my divorce when he was two, and of how his father treats him? People have always bullied him, girls won't go out with him, and teachers don't like him. My fear is that he's going to kill himself one day if he doesn't get relief or kill someone else out of anguish. What are we supposed to do?"

I believe that most young people who go on a rampage, shooting others in malls or schools, do so because of a combination of two things: hopelessness in their current situation and a sense of abandonment by others. It's an attempt to "pay back" mankind for their misery, forcing others to feel a similar hurt to what they have been carrying for years. An understanding of what is driving these young people to plan and carry out mass murder can help bring sense into the senselessness and a plan to help insure it doesn't happen with a teenager you know—especially your own.

I always wince a little right before a newscaster shares the name of any shooter who took out his aggression, anger, or disappointment with life through the senseless killing of many at a mall, school or a church. I wince not just because I have a tough time hearing of such a tragic event, but also because I worry that in the next second I may hear the name of a young person from a family I know. I meet and get to know families from all over. Some of these families include teens who have such pain, anger and hopelessness that I am astonished they can still breathe, let alone function.

I wonder about the nineteen-year-old kid in Omaha, Nebraska, and what his motivation was to shoot and kill nine innocent people and injure several others in a crowded mall on December 5, 2007 – the deadliest mall shooting in US history. Did anyone sense that something like this could happen? Where were the shooter's friends? Where were Mom and Dad? Why did he feel that the killing of others would compensate for loss in his own life? Where did his hopelessness and rage come from?

Don't you find yourself asking the same questions, trying to "make sense" of it all?

After such shootings, many of the comments from friends of the shooter sound the same, all saying in some form, "*I never knew that this person could do this...*" or, "*We did all the right things... How could this have happened?*" or "*This young man was basically a good kid, how could he have...?*" These are questions that we probably won't know the answer to this side of heaven. But I'm convinced of this: We live in a hurting world that hurts people. And hurt people hurt other people.

Hurt people hurt people. And if we can help those who hurt, it will stop them from hurting others.

Hopelessness is a tough state of mind to be in, no matter who you are. If depression is left unchecked, it can easily progress to hopelessness. Hopelessness can lead to suicidal thoughts and even contempt for others. In a state of depression, people just don't think well. They feel isolated. They feel that no one likes them. They feel "dark." They are sometimes consumed with irrational thoughts like, "*Why was I even born?*" or, "*I'm nothing but a failure.*" Left alone and untreated, these people can justify just about anything... ending their own life, an uncaring attitude about others' lives, and a mind-set that "things will only get worse, so why not?" It's a tough place to be.

If those thoughts are fueled by the unkind actions of others, whether actual or perceived, that can be enough to send a depressed and hopeless person over the edge. As rare as these incidents are, they capture our hearts and attention, and should cause us all to reflect on what could have been done to prevent such tragedies, since in many more cases that we don't hear about, the hopeless teenager simply ends his own life without fanfare.

I am sure that I have met many young people just like the kids who become shooters in mass tragedies. Had they not worked through their "issues" and developed new coping skills in our Heartlight program, it would not have surprised me to hear their names on such a newscast. I know, because I have sat and talked with them for hours, weeks and months, helping them through it—helping them get to the other side.

It's true that there are people who have psychological issues far beyond the common person's ability to help them. In most cases, these issues are quite apparent, and good doctors and medications can help, but there are many more people, and teenagers in particular, who silently struggle. If we never try to reach out to those silent, struggling ones, they will continue down their dark paths. Look for the teen who always seems to be hiding in the corner, the girl who is promiscuous, the young man who participates in more and more life-threatening behaviors – extreme sports, mimicking violent behaviors and stunts, etc. Talk to these teens. Let them know that you are there for them. Listen to them. They are telling you so much, especially when they are not speaking! There is probably more going on than simply teen angst.

"Faithless is he who disappears when the road is dark."[1] –J.R.R. Tolkien

If you think you cannot help a teen through such a situation, let me assure you that it doesn't take a degree or some great skill. Don't get me wrong. It is not easy. It takes heart and strength and stick-to-itive-ness that is hard to maintain. It takes a "with-you-no-matter-what-ness"…being with someone as she struggles through tough times, in order to bring light to those dark places. You need an extra dose of patience and love when dealing with hopeless teens. For every step forward, there will probably be three backwards. They expect you to give up on them. In their minds, everybody else has already given up on them (even themselves), so why should you be any different? It is a very slow journey from hopelessness to hopefulness.

If you are depressed yourself, or worse, hopeless, then you must get help for yourself. If you have no light within yourself, how can you bring light into the life of your teen?

Here are a few ways to bring light to the life of a hopeless teenager:

1. **Brush off the Push-Off.**—Don't give in to a teen's attempt to keep you away. Always offer yourself in ways that let a young person know there is nothing he can do to push you away. Even if you simply sit quietly next to him, keep showing your teen that you are there, ready to listen, always loving him! This takes a willingness to meet teens where they are. If you have a need for people around you always to be happy, this is going to be extremely difficult for you. Hopeless teens are angry, contemptuous, and apathetic. You need to be willing to stand in the midst of that mess of human darkness.

There's a deodorant slogan that says you should never let anyone see you sweat. Apply it here. Teens can easily sense your discomfort. They may incorrectly identify the emotion or motivation behind it, but they can tell when adults are uncomfortable. They will try to use this against you in their attempts to push you away. Stand firm, reassuring them that, though you may be uncomfortable, you are willing to stand with them in this darkness until the light can penetrate it!

2. **Just Listen.**—Spend time "being" rather than "fixing." Be with them, and don't try to fix everything. Be quick to listen, slow to speak, and don't get mad when they say things that are sharp or confused. Teens will constantly say things to "test" the adults who are trying to help them. They believe that everybody will hurt them in some way, abandon them, or stop loving them. Hurting

teens will say some very hurtful and cruel things to "prove" that their fears are real, their assumption that everyone is out to get them is correct. Don't take the bait. Prove them wrong. Love them. Listen to them. Be intentional in your actions, not reactive. The key is to "Stop, think, go."

Being there to listen as they throw all their confused thoughts at you will help them to process much of what is going on in their minds and hearts. If you keep interrupting and trying to fix things, they will not learn how to work through difficult emotions and bad situations. You are robbing them of growth opportunities every time you jump in and try to solve their problems. Loving teens means being willing to let them work things out for themselves. Don't emotionally step away; just stand beside them as they work through this. Offer advice only when they ask for it. Being a good listener is difficult for most people. It takes intentionality and practice to keep quiet when someone is hurting.

3. **Encourage Help.**—Encourage teens to accept the help of others. Counselors, doctors, therapists, pastors, teachers, school staff, and even law enforcement if things get beyond what you think you can handle. Just don't give up. Hang in there with them. The reason many people don't reach out for help is because that action would confirm in their own minds that there is something wrong with them. There is a lot of shame attached to mental health issues in this country. Society tells us that it is a sign of weakness not to be able to handle life alone. This is such an unrealistic expectation, since nobody can go through life handling everything by himself.

We are so uncomfortable with negative emotions that we try to pretend they don't really exist. We demand quick fixes for everything from weight loss to depression. Commercials tout the next miracle drug to cure depression, insomnia, obesity, nicotine addiction, and on and on it goes. Instant gratification also makes the process harder. If teens don't feel better quickly (in a matter of days), they give up. "See, I told you it was useless," they may say. Any way that you can, help them feel and understand that it's okay not to have it all together. The best way to transfer this concept is to let them know that you don't have it all together either. Keep telling them that there is no shame in feeling the way they feel. There is no shame in asking for and getting help.

4. **Be Watchful.**—If you see something that is suspect, get other people involved. Don't just ignore what your heart or eyes are telling you. If you see that one of the teens in your church is always sitting alone, pull the youth director aside. Mention your observation in private. He might be aware of something, or he may be too busy corralling the rest of the energetic teens to have noticed.

Now I'm not saying that you should be paranoid about everything you see or become a busybody. Don't be like Mrs. Gladys Kravitz from the old *Bewitched* TV series. Do you remember her? She was always staring out her curtains at the neighbors and gossiping about everything she saw to her husband, Abner. I am convinced that there are many people out there who would welcome a helping hand to literally cling to as they walk through their struggles.

5. **Keep with It.**—Stay in the relationship for the long haul. Hurt people take time to heal. Let them know that you will walk with them on the long walk, not just the short stroll. Don't abandon them. A huge part of how the hurting person got where they are is a sense of abandonment by those he or she cares about – and whether it is actual or perceived is of no consequence. Whatever is perceived is reality to that person. There is no quick fix. Healing takes time. You need to be willing to invest yourself in this relationship for however long as it takes. If you abandon the hurting teen during the process, you just reinforce the belief that she is worthless and nobody could ever love her. Stay connected. Stay involved. Keep loving her.

The Good News of Christ is not only found in His Word, but also through the actions of those who love Him. For young people around us who are hurting, we are to beckon them to come to us when they are weary and heavy-laden. Such undying love on our part, consistently applied and never withheld, sends a message that "fleshes out" the gospel to hurting young people and points them to the hope found in Christ. Without the hope of Christ, a sense of hopelessness cannot be lifted. We are each called to share that hope. The Son of God died for each and every one of us. He rose again and lives today. There is hope. There is peace. Through Jesus, we all will be healed and made whole. If we, as Christians, are not living each day with this Truth in our hearts and our heads, how are we to offer hope to the hopeless?

If this life was meant to be easy, Scripture wouldn't have to talk about having the grace of God, the strength of God, or the peace of God. The New Testament has so many wonderful statements of God's character and promises for trying times. In Ephesians, Paul writes about putting on the full "armor" of God. He urges each of us to daily clothe ourselves with the armor of God to protect us from the pain and evil of this world. We need the protection of God to get through each and every day. Here are some of God's promises to us:

> *"Stand firm then, with the belt of truth buckled around your waist, with the breastplate of righteousness in place, and with your feet fitted with the readiness that comes from the gospel of peace. In addition to all this, take up the shield of faith, with which you can extinguish all the flaming arrows of the evil one. Take the helmet of salvation and the sword of the Spirit, which is the word of God."* (Ephesians 6:14-17, NIV)

Jesus said,

> *"Do not let your hearts be troubled. Trust in God; trust also in me."* (John 14:1, NIV)

The Old Testament promises,

> *"Because of the LORD's great love we are not consumed, for his compassions never fail. They are new every morning; great is your faithfulness. I say to myself, "The LORD is my portion; therefore I will wait for him." The LORD is good to those whose hope is in him, to the one who seeks him."* (Lamentations 3:22-25, NIV)

Bringing light to dark situations with teenagers is what our full-time Heartlight residential program in East Texas is all about. We've helped thousands of kids get to the other side of such issues, and I cannot help but wonder what kind of trouble those kids would have gotten into had they not received the kind of love and treatment we provide. Many of them later say, "I'd be dead today had I not gone to Heartlight," and their parents and friends usually echo that sentiment.

The question is: Would they have taken anyone else with them? If you know of a young person who is struggling, please tell their parents or counselor about Heartlight. From the full-time residential counseling program to various books, audio and video training resources, we provide many ways to help teens in crisis.

When Do We Take Action, and When Do We Wait?

Questions are often sent to our office everyday from parents seeking help with their particular issues and asking for direction and guidance. There are times that we can, from a broad point of view, answer many of the questions. And that's what I've attempted to do throughout this book. Yet there are some that cannot be answered with a general answer because of the intensity of the situation and the out-of-control environment in which the family finds itself. Instead of trying to blindly answer each one of these, I've decided to list some examples of the types of questions sent to us that can be answered with a broad answer that could appropriately pertain to each. If you are in one of these situations, I think you'll be able to identify with the pain and find hope in the answers.

> *"We are dealing with many issues involving lack of respect, rebellion, trouble in school (failing for second year in a row), no respect for authority or rules (nothing legal yet), and a lot of passive-aggressive behavior. Our child is on his way to trouble with the law or teen pregnancy really soon. We have tried counseling for years, involved the school, talked to our pastor and anyone we can. However, the cycle of negative outcomes continues. We have nothing left to use for consequences. He doesn't care about anything. He is only passing one class at school and is even failing two gym classes. Gym class! How do you flunk that? Every week we go through a cycle of*

*his breaking the rules and our trying to come up with
consequences for his actions as he tells us, "What are you
going to do about it?" and "I'll do what I want." In the
meantime, he is not breaking the law yet, so we have no
recourse. He will be seventeen soon and has threatened to
leave home many times. I fear for what will then happen.
I have reached out to every resource I can think of and
am desperate for help. Can you help us?"*

*"Megan has always been very precocious, inquisitive and
sensitive. She has experienced a number of losses during
her early years, including the death of my mother and my
brother (who was her favorite family member). Year after
year, at school she lost friends, either to moves or because
of social issues. Fifth grade was awful. She entered sixth
grade and seemed to be fine. Seventh found her turning
toward the computer (MySpace and Goth influences).
We are Christians and believe Megan is, too, but she
seemed to be less interested in God, as she didn't think
He cared about her or was doing anything for her. In
ninth grade she decided that she wasn't thin enough to be
attractive, so she lost too much weight and was anorexic
for a short while. We took her to a counselor for this,
but Megan lied to the counselor and convinced her there
was nothing wrong. She hated school and begged for us
to move, which we were considering anyway. She wanted
to start over in a new situation. She also began cutting.
We started taking her to a different counselor who is a
Christian. We moved and Megan hated it even worse
than the old school. The cutting continued. We took
her to a psychiatrist who prescribed medication for her
depression. Megan then met Marcus, who encouraged
her to skip school. She started sneaking out at night. She
is seriously depressed due to another horrendous school
situation from this past fall. She is failing three of her
classes. She feels she has no friends, which is close to the
truth. Marcus is her boyfriend of almost a year, and they
fight more than anything else. Yet she can't give him up,
because she would have no one to socialize with. She is*

still seeing the counselor. She feels that she has no life now and no future to even think about. I'm just grateful she hasn't committed suicide. I think that is by the grace of God. What are we to do?"

"Jason will be sixteen in June. He is rebellious and disobedient much of the time, while occasionally he obeys in a timely manner. He became sexually involved about six months ago, which has made things more difficult. In speaking with a couple of our pastors at church, including Jason's youth pastor, we have been advised that he might need a change of pace and environment to mature. It has been a tremendous strain on our marriage of twenty-two years and on our fourteen-year-old son. Jason does not want to go away, but he doesn't want to change enough to follow the rules. Is there something that we can do, or are we stuck?"

My daughter Kit is a beautiful, very intelligent young lady. She is thirteen years old. She has scars all over her arms, legs and side from cutting herself. What started, I think, as a fad, has tragically turned into an addiction of self-abuse in an attempt to cope. Her father and I were divorced a few years ago. He was an alcoholic who suffered from depression and later committed suicide. It has been a turning point in her life, and I believe that she has lost any hope she had in herself. She has been seeing a Christian counselor, after a brief hospital stay. Somewhere beneath all her "stuff," she is a wonderful girl. I just got her leg stitched from another cut. She has become a very good liar; so good that she convinces me and others many times. I know that she needs help, the help that only God can give her. She just needs to let Him! How do we get her to that point?"

"My eighteen-year-old son was in residential treatment for attachment disorder and emotional problems a couple of years ago. He did well for about a year after that. Unfortunately, he has once again become involved with old friends and is spiraling downhill. He is supposed to be graduating in a couple of weeks. This past week, he

stole my credit card and drove to Alabama with a friend of his who is already on probation. He calls us every foul name in the book and says that he can do what he wants because he is eighteen. We are at a loss as to what to do with him. He was raised in a Christian home and wants nothing to do with God or us. We feel like our hands are tied. Should we kick him out?"

"Our daughter is becoming increasingly resistant to our household rules. Teachers at her Christian school are concerned over the lack of respect they see developing. When she gets angry at home, and this is often, she throws huge fits of screaming and threatening. Yesterday, she bashed her dad's head—an injury that required stitches. When we removed the computer, she blamed us for ruining her life and put some holes in the walls using her foot. We learned that she is "cutting," and though she says she isn't doing this anymore, we discovered last night that she told a friend she was thinking about it again. We have attempted to get her help. She feels she doesn't need help, and all of her bad choices are our fault. She is often out of control with her anger, and this is causing a lot of stress in our home. There is great stress between her and her three siblings. She is becoming physically abusive and very verbally abusive toward her eleven-year-old brother. Our youngest often says she's afraid of her because of her yelling and fits. She has been in a loving Christian school. Because she is shy, she has had difficulty feeling like she fit in until the past few weeks. Everything in her life is "stupid," including most authorities and people she has loved forever. As far as we know, there has been no substance abuse. Thankfully, she has some very good Christian friends she shares with. She tells her friends her "stuff," and they have a heart to help her. She says we don't know the half of what she's dealing with, yet she refuses to share with us. Do we just leave her alone and let her grow out of it?"

"I have been noticing some of the warning signs that were in an e-mail you sent… falling and failing grades, lack of *respect, uncontrollable anger, mood swings, and loss of interest in things my son once loved. Last week I found a bag of pills in his room. I confronted him, and he told me not to worry, that he would be dead by morning. I took him to the emergency room, and they found three other prescription drugs in his system, one of which was mine. In his system, they didn't find any of the medications that were in the bag. Much to my dismay, they sent him home. I took him to his doctor the next day. I don't even know how many doctors, counselors, psychologists, and pastors I've called now trying to get him in for help. I keep getting the response, "We can't get him in until next month at the earliest." I'm getting absolutely nowhere. I have told the school that kids are passing these pills around in the parking lot and everywhere they can. Michael has told me that he doesn't believe in God. He says that he doesn't even believe in religion. He has been telling me that for a very long time. I realize that I have done so many things wrong and just don't know what to do here. I want to help my son, and I don't know how. Do you have any direction for me?"*

"William is chronically abusing marijuana, as well as trying other drugs on occasion, skipping school, getting poor grades, having no motivation, and stealing. I'm afraid the problems will get worse if they are not addressed. We tried weekly therapy for a short duration, but that proved to be ineffective, as William lied to the therapist. William is still warm-hearted and open to a certain degree. What are we supposed to do?"

"Our son is a Christian. He is not rebellious, but he is lost, confused, and scared. He has been battling self-mutilation and has been in weekly therapy for about six months. His latest "slip" required an emergency room trip and eight stitches. His therapist wants him to take antidepressants, but he has refused. Though open to talking with us about this issue, he's also vaguely referenced that there is "more" but refuses to go any deeper. Last night I think the "more" was revealed when

my husband caught him on a porn site, and Adam (our son) admitted addiction. Our third concern is that Adam loves writing and shows talent, but his stories now are so dark, gruesome, and even spiritually evil. We are becoming increasingly concerned that Adam is wearying of the battle and turmoil and may just opt for suicide. I feel we're at least at the 'urgent' point. Can you help?"

"Our sixteen-year-old, Beth, was adopted from El Salvador at the age of six, the oldest of a sibling group we adopted. Since she was fourteen, she has been sneaking out of the house at night, sometimes staying out all night. She was in an alternative school and was asked to leave the school because of plagiarism and refusal to do some of the work. She has experimented to some extent with alcohol, drugs, and cigarettes, but two drug tests have shown her to be drug-free. She has stolen money from us and probably from other people. She consistently lies. She can appear sweet, compliant and cooperative, but more and more she is acting out in dangerous ways. She is scheduled to have her wisdom teeth out, and the dentist gave her a prescription for painkillers. Shortly afterwards, we found that thirteen of the twenty pills were missing. She said she gave them to a friend. Her behavior is monopolizing our time as parents and worrying her siblings, neither of whom displays the lack of attachment, feelings of unworthiness, or acting out behavior that Beth does. Both my husband and I are strong Christians. Beth attends church and Sunday school and frequently goes to Young Life. We let her go to a club last night from nine to eleven o'clock, but when my husband went to pick her up she was not there or would not come even though they paged her. We did not hear from her until four-thirty a.m., when she called me and asked me to pick her up from a mall. She did not explain where she had been or what she had been doing. Is this normal for an adopted kid?"

"My daughter has steadfastly become more aggressive, refuses to reason, and seems to have no differentiation

between right and wrong. She chooses to do whatever she wants. She is failing school and does not care about anything anymore. She is completely boy-crazy, and her behavior continues to deteriorate. My husband and I are truly out of ideas, consequences and plans. We don't know what to do to get through to her and help her! Can you help us?"

"My son has gone from being a faith-based person to someone who is just totally lost and not himself. He has no interest in ANYTHING anymore. He wants to sleep all the time and does not want to go to school or church. His friends are leading him down paths of unhappiness, and he just seems to become more and more broken inside. Our family is worried we may lose him if we don't try to help him. A babysitter sexually abused him when he was younger, and he has cut and burned himself. He drinks to try to deal with his pain. He has had counseling, and it has not been successful. I do not want to send him away or get help from just anywhere. I know he needs help now, and I cannot put this off. Please show me where and what to do. I have tried everything I know for this child. I know he is still reachable. He is very impressionable. He just needs the right people in his life to point the way and the right environment. He has a great heart in there somewhere. He has had a tough life. He doesn't fit in well and has been bullied also. I am sending this as my cry for help and my prayer. Please, please, please..."

I usually don't ever say "You need to..." as part of my directives to families who are struggling. My thought is that they don't *need* to do anything, if that's what they choose. However, in the above situations I will say that *you need to do something* in these kinds of cases. Too many times, I've seen a lack of parental action end with horrific consequences. You need to get help for your situation beyond the current, failing strategy of dealing with your teen. Each of these stories has disaster written all over it! Should the behavior of any of these teens be allowed to continue, the prognosis for resolution, in my opinion, would be grim. Extreme out-of-control behavior demands extreme solution tactics.

Most of these issues, because of their extreme nature, are not going to be resolved at home. Sending your child off is not the only thing you can do when they're spinning out of control. I would encourage you to try a number of different things first. But the resolution might include a residential treatment center like Heartlight, drug treatment, a therapeutic boarding school, hospitalization, a wilderness camp, a relative or close friend's home, or telling a teen he must live elsewhere until issues can be resolved or the teen comes to his or her senses.

I believe in counseling, but I would not recommend counseling alone without a restructuring of the home environment that would enforce boundaries, demand respect, and provide for the safety of all family members. I believe in prayer, and I would suggest that all involve pray, while searching for new ways that God will use to intervene in the life of your teen and your entire family. I believe in the hand of God working in the life of your child. And while His hand is working, I would strongly urge you to be using your hands to find solutions as well.

One of the biggest concerns shared about finding alternative places for a teen to live is the expense of such programs. I know that all of the alternatives I suggested above, short of a child living with other relatives or friends or being forced to live on his own, are expensive. Many say they can't afford to spend the money. I would suggest that they can't afford not to. This might be the time to spend a child's college fund money. It might be a time to ask other family members to help. It might be necessary to take out educational loans, or a second mortgage on a home. It's time to ask your church, your Sunday school class, or your employer to help. I say all these things because I hear teens say all the time that had they not gotten help, they think they would be dead.

As a part of Heartlight Ministries, we hold retreats, put on conferences, write books, produce curriculum, and air a radio program to provide resources for families. Many times parents tell me, "I appreciate all the information, but this is my child's problem, not mine." To that I say, "It is your teen's problem, but whether your teen pulls out of the mess depends on how you approach your child." That is what all of our resources are about—helping parents cope and deal with that teen who is struggling. Are you willing to put forth your resources to save your teen—and restore your family?

Are these serious issues? You bet. So approach them with the most delicate of detail, and with every resource needed to move them to resolution. What you might save in the process is your child's life.

Where Is the Line Between Accountability and Grace?

"It's becoming harder and harder to give my child something she doesn't deserve because she is so demanding. It seems like she is always asking for more and never satisfied with what she gets. She makes it difficult to want to offer her anything. I find myself even wanting to withdraw my relationship with her because she is so self-centered and self-absorbed. How does grace fit in with a child who deserves nothing?"

When teenagers' behaviors are way out of line, when they cross established boundaries and offend us and make us angry, it is easy to think they don't deserve grace. But that may be exactly the right time to give it. The very definition of grace is that it is undeserved consideration. Undeserved forgiveness, undeserved privileges, undeserved love. Grace is *always* undeserved—when we give it or receive it.

Grace, given at just the right moment, has the power to change the direction of any struggle and may ultimately bring it to an end. Grace can bring healing, restoration, and a new direction to your teens' path.

A biblical definition of grace is this: *God's undeserved favor and forgiveness when we've chosen to do the unforgivable.* In human terms, grace is an act of kindness, love, and forgiveness in the face of bad behavior or poor choices. For your teens, those bad behaviors and choices can be outright rebellion and rotten attitudes. We are each called to be the hands and feet of God. That means we are called to act with love and grace.

Now I am not saying that all your teen's transgressions should be ignored as a sign of your grace. No! You have to allow the consequences of bad behavior to be felt. For example, if one of your family rules is that the car is not to be out past curfew, and the agreed-upon consequence is loss of that car for one week for the first offense, take the car away for a week the first time your teens come home late. You allow the consequences to be felt – take their keys, tell them they have to take the bus, walk, find a ride to work, school, or whatever for one week. You can show grace to your teens by giving them a ride (not by giving the keys back). If you choose to give them a ride, you need to do so joyfully. Grace given grudgingly with discontent and anger is not grace at all.

I recently worked with a teen who rarely received grace at home. He was angry all the time and spewed anger on everyone and everything around him, including the side of my van. Instead of having him arrested for bashing my vehicle with a baseball bat, I sat him down and told him he was forgiven, he wouldn't be arrested, and that we were going to work things out differently from now on. He was still responsible for his actions and had consequences he had to face – yard duty, loss of privileges, having to apologize for his anger and his behavior.

As we began to talk, tears came to his eyes. He had never experienced that kind of forgiveness in the face of his anger, and he couldn't believe I didn't have the police waiting to take him to jail. Giving him grace, at just the right moment, went a long way to change the direction he was headed. In the end, after a lot of work, he successfully completed the Heartlight program.

How do you know exactly the right time to extend grace? How about when it is least deserved? I guess that's how you'll know it's grace - because it won't feel good. In fact, it may be enough to put you in a really bad mood. I didn't enjoy having a smashed-in van. I didn't like having to pay for the repairs. But that's the nature of grace. It doesn't feel good when you're giving it, it costs you, but you are never more like Christ than when you offer it.

As believers, we should understand grace-giving. After all, didn't God love us so much that while we were sinners He sent His Son to die for us? He took our place for the penalty of our sin. He paid the ultimate price for our mistakes and shortcomings. God, His Father, paid dearly to save those He created – each of us. Can you even imagine the pain and sorrow God felt when He allowed His Son to be nailed to the cross? You know He hurt. I bet He cried heaving sobs as His Son died. Did He yell at us, call us names, and then give us grace? No. Did He demand anything in return? Not really. That kind of grace, true grace, didn't come easily, and we should learn from it and imitate it. When you decide to offer grace to your teens, don't be stingy about it. Don't demand anything because of it. It is okay to let them see that you are upset and sad about their behaviors, but it is never okay to call them names, cause shame, or degrade them.

It is not easy to receive grace, either. We all know that. We all have been in situations where we have received grace and have been very uncomfortable and shamed by our behavior. We have been overwhelmed with a sense of confusion and gratitude at receiving grace. Your teen will experience that when you offer grace. She may even try to throw it back in your face because of her emotional turmoil. Do not let her discomfort detract from the lesson at hand. Be gentle as you explain why you are offering grace in this situation. Reiterate it as often as needed. Remind your teen that there is nothing, NOTHING, that can make you love her more or love her less.

Walk softly, love loudly! Your teens need you to love them no matter what. Grace helps them see that they can do nothing to change your love for them.

Giving grace in parenting doesn't mean we allow bad behavior to continue unchecked. That's not grace. That's enabling or empowering our child to keep up bad behavior without fear of consequences. As I've talked about many times, the pain of consequences is what causes all of us to take notice of our bad behavior - so we make a change. Some say that pain is a terrible part of God's creation, but the fact is, without it we'd never change. Pain keeps us in check and tells us when something is wrong. The great author C. S. Lewis called pain "God's megaphone." [1] Nothing gets our attention quicker than pain – physical or emotional.

As children, we learned very quickly not to touch the burners on the stove after grabbing hold of a hot one. If you ever stuck a metal object in a wall socket as a child, I would bet you never did it more than once! Pain gets our attention and teaches us a lesson each and every time. The Apostle Paul spoke many times of the constant pain he had; he compared it to a thorn in his side. Though we really have no clear idea of what that pain was, we do know that Paul prayed often for God to remove it, and God never did. We also know that Paul decided to be grateful for that pain despite the discomfort it brought. He chose to believe that God had a specific reason for not removing it. Though we may not be able to understand why, God has a reason for the pain in your life, the struggles you are going through with your teen. Are you looking up to God for support, healing and guidance, or are you curled in a fetal position moaning about how unfair life is?

Giving grace isn't always popular. Remember that story of the sibling in the story of the prodigal son? He questioned his father's decision to extend grace to his brother. After all, he had stayed behind to help the family while the prodigal was off seeking pleasure. Even though the decision was unpopular, the father gave grace—and he gave it wholeheartedly. Did he wait for his wayward son to reach the porch, apologize and ask for forgiveness? No. He ran to the gate, threw it open, gathered his son in his arms and hugged him! Did this act of grace by the father enable the prodigal's behavior? Not in the least, because the prodigal had already experienced the natural consequences for his poor choices and bad behaviors – poverty, loss of possessions, and loss of dignity were all severe consequences. Did the father have to allow his son to come home? Of course not, but the father saw what was important. His son was home, their relationship could be restored, and his family could be whole again.

What about the older son who had stayed and continued to work for the father? Was he as excited about his brother's return? Not even close. Having his father offer grace to his younger brother must have been like a slap in the face to him. His younger brother had already blown through half of everything his father had built within his lifetime, had broken his father's heart and skipped off to live in ignorant bliss of the turmoil left in his wake. What was to stop him from doing it all over again? The older brother was full of resentment that the younger one got to go "play" while he stayed and continued to work hard and obey his father. The older son, the "good" son, had a heart filled with resentment and discontent, but no courage to do anything about it. He demanded an explanation from his father for giving such a lavish party for the younger son, having so far refused to join the family and friends. He begrudges all the things his father has given the prodigal upon his return – the finest robe, a ring for his finger (very likely something of gold with precious stones) to show wealth and favor, and shoes for his feet (not everyone had shoes in Biblical times). "It's not FAIR!" his brain shouts. He pouts that he has never been given even a baby goat, so that he and his friends could have a party.

Do you know what his father said? He said that everything he owned had always been there for the good son to use as if it were his own. The good son never saw that one coming, I bet! Too bad we don't get to hear how the rest of the evening went. I think, after digesting what his father said to him, the good son asked forgiveness and joined the party with the rest of the family.

Remember, Grace...

- Is most often needed when it is least deserved.
- Does not directly benefit the giver.
- Will often be misunderstood by others.
- Doesn't enable bad behavior to continue.
- Is best when it is offered at just the right time.
- Comes from a desire for a new direction, an understanding of your child's heart, and his need to be restored.

We are never more like Christ than when we give our teen grace in the face of a struggle. Giving grace when it surely is not deserved may change the direction of the struggle, or even bring it to an end.

Closing

In closing, let me ask you a question: Did you pick this book up with the hopes of finding some new "list" that, if followed, would solve all the issues with your teen? Let me assure you of something. That list doesn't exist. A list confines the solution of any individual issue to a "rubber stamp answer" for the masses. I just don't think that God is like that.

I grew up in an era when people were told that God had an individual plan for each of our lives. I was taught that each person is as unique as the fingerprints stamped on their digits—in order to express the uniqueness of their hearts. I was told that God wanted a personal relationship with me. And I was told that I was uniquely created, fearfully and wonderfully made, and that Christ died for *me*. I was told that I was precious in God's sight.

Those Truths that I heard I passed on to my children. I worked hard as a young dad to help my children hear the concept of God's love for them and desire to be in personal relationship with them. I told them of the uniqueness of their souls, and how they, too, were fearfully and wonderfully made. I let them know that Christ had an individual plan for their lives.

I'm sure you did the same.

Then came the adolescent years.

Just because there is conflict during these years, or because there might be some challenges faced with the raising of your teen, the uniqueness of your teen is not negated. Nor is the uniqueness of his conflict, or the uniqueness of the answers needed for the questions that you are asking about your current situation. To think a "list" will answer every question staring you in the face would be foolish thinking.

I hope what you found throughout the questions and answers in this book is a mind-set, a framework that can be adapted to your family. Throughout these chapters, I tried to give an understanding of the path to find the answer, rather than to give you numbered steps to take for instant resolution.

Years ago, a wise lady was teaching me how to break and train horses. She explained that she wasn't going to give me a step-by-step plan to break and train every horse in the world. She explained to me that every horse was unique, and she was going to help me understand horses (in general) and teach me how they thought. From that basis, I would be able to find solutions to all the questions that would arise from my working with horses. I think this approach works equally well with teens.

There is a two-step challenge to applying the answers in this book to your situation with your pre-adolescent or teen. First, it is understanding your teen. Second, you can then spend time adapting, combining, and refining the broad answers to similar questions you might be asking, in such a way that they would be effective in the life of your teen.

It's hard work. There's no easy answer. And there's no easy remedy. But the process is worthwhile. In your journey to find good answers to the hard questions that you have, you will find that God indeed is involved in your life and the life of your teen, even when you don't have a clue to His direction or feel a touch of His presence.

May God continue to use you in a mighty way to offer to your teen a taste of His character. My prayer for you is that you would get a glimpse of "the bigger picture" of the adolescent years of your teen's life, and know that all you do for your teen during these years does not go unnoticed... by Him, or by your teen.

NOTES

Question 5

1. Page 55 - Internet Addiction: Stanford Study Seeks To Define Whether It's A Problem *ScienceDaily (Oct. 17, 2006)* Stanford University School of Medicine

Question 6

1. Page 60 - The Essential Reinhold Niebuhr: Selected Essays and Addresses, editor: Robert McAfee Brown *The International Journal of Alcoholics Anonymous*, identified Niebuhr as the author (January 1950, pp. 6-7),
2. Page 67 - *Sex in the Body of Christ*, Lauren F. Winner. Christianity Today, May 2005.

Question 7

1. Page 73 – Mark Gregston's Interview with Jason Illian, Heartlight Radio, *"The Internet and Your Teen"*, program # 54. Jason is author of *"MySpace, My Kids"*.

Question 9

1. Page 85 - *Dictionary.com Unabridged (v 1.1) Based on the Random House Unabridged Dictionary, © Random House, Inc. 2006. And Online Etymology Dictionary, ©* 2001 Douglas Harper
2. Page 86 – Mark Gregston Interview with Dr. Tim Kimmel, Heartlight Radio, *"Shifting our Styles of Parenting,"* Program # 49. Tim is the author of *"Grace Based Parenting."*

Question 15

1. Page 127 – Mark Gregston Interview with Dr. Melody Rhode, Heartlight Radio, "Author of Reconciliation," Program # 58. Dr. Rhode is Licensed Clinical Psychologist in Bellingham, Washington.

Question 18

1. Page 147 - *Protecting Children from Sexual Predators: SB 132* Attorney General Roy Cooper July 24, 2007. North Carolina Department of Justice.

Question 20

1. Page 159 – American Association of Christian Counselors Annual Convention, Nashville, Tennessee September 2007. In conjunction with an interview with Mark Gregston on Heartlight Radio's weekly program titled "When Teens Shatter Your Dreams, aired September 15, 2007, Program # 37.

Question 22

1. Page 176 – Henry Cloud and John Townsend, *Boundaries* (Grand Rapids: Zondervan, 1992), p. 78.

Question 29

1. Page 236 - *Dictionary.com Unabridged (v 1.1) Based on the Random House Unabridged Dictionary,* © *Random House, Inc. 2006.*

Question 30

1. Page 243 – J.R.R. Tolkien, *The Fellowship of the Ring* (New York: Houghton Mifflin, 2004), p. 348

Question 32

1. Page 262 – C.S. Lewis, *The Problem of Pain* (New York: HarperCollins, 2001), p. 91

MARK GREGSTON, has worked with teens and their families for the past 34 years, beginning his ministry in Tulsa, Oklahoma. He has served as a youth minister, an Area Director with Young Life, and has been involved in adolescent residential counseling the last 26 years.

Mark and his wife of 33 years, Jan, founded Heartlight Ministries in 1988 and have had over 2,000 teens live with them since that time.

The Heartlight Radio weekend show is heard on over 450 stations across the country and the short feature daily program, Parenting Today's Teens is heard on over 2,500 outlets.

In addition to the Heartlight Residential Counseling Ministry and the Heartlight Radio programs, Mark leads weekend parenting seminars, Dealing With Today's Teens. He has also authored several books and booklets which include *When Your Teen is Struggling, What's Happening to My Teen, A Look at the Other Side of Adoption, When Your Prodigal Won't Leave Home, and The Internet and your Teen.* His small group curriculum, Dealing With Today's Teens, is taught in hundreds of churches across the country.

When Mark isn't speaking around the country, he spends time in the country at home in Texas with his two grown kids, his son in law, and his 2 grandchildren.

Endorsements

Do you ever wonder if today's teen culture will affect your child? Have you seen the effects of this confusing culture on your teen? Are you as confused trying to navigate in these waters called adolescence?

Teen Expert Mark Gregston answers 32 of the toughest questions asked by parents today concerning their teen, and gives solid insight and practical wisdom as to how to approach your teen during the time of their life that they need you the most. Mark shares his stories of over 2,000 teens that have lived with him, and the lessons that he has learned from his involvement in their life. Whether you have a teen who is struggling, fearful that your teen might struggle when they enter the teen years, or just want to prepare now for those often turbulent years, this book is for you.

 **MARK GREGSTON** is the radio host of *Heartlight Radio's* weekend program, and also heard on hundreds of stations with their daily program, *Parenting Today's Teens.* He is the founder and Executive Director of Heartlight, a residential counseling center for teens in crisis, and is the author of several books and workbooks. A popular speaker and seminar leader, Mark blends his humor and storytelling with Biblical insights that touch the heart of parents wanting a deep relationship with their teen. Mark and his wife Jan have been married for 34 years, have two children, two grandchildren, four dogs, and way too many horses.

Heartlight Ministries
FOUNDATION

P. O. Box 480 Hallsville, Texas 75650
www.HeartlightResources.com

ISBN: 978-0-615-24835-6   # $14.99

More Trusted Resources From Teen Parenting Expert Mark Gregston

A broad spectrum of helps and resources are available to parents and youth workers from *Heartlight Ministries*...

Printed, Audio and Video Resources

Heartlight Resources
www.heartlightresources.com

National Radio

The Voice of Heartlight – *1-hour weekly radio program*
www.heartlightradio.org

Parenting Today's Teens – *1-minute daily radio spots*
www.parentingtodaysteens.org

Counseling and Coaching

Heartlight Residential Program for Teens
www.heartlightministries.org

Family Crisis Coaching – *coaching by phone*
www.familycrisiscoaching.com

Conferences

Dealing With Today's Teens – *small group & church conferences*
www.dealingwithtodaysteens.org

Families in Crisis Conference – *a weekend on-campus retreat*
www.familycrisisconference.com

Online Articles

Parenting Today's Teens – *blog and articles by email*
www.markgregston.com

Teen Parenting Tips – *daily teen parenting tips*
www.parentingteentips.com

Radio Programs Online
www.heartlightradioonline.com

Heartlight

RESIDENTIAL COUNSELING CENTER FOR TEENS

For more information
about Heartlight, or to
receive an admission packet,
please call 903.668.2173
or visit our website at
www.HeartlightMinistries.org

AN ATMOSPHERE OF
relationships

Nestled among the beautiful piney woods of East Texas, Heartlight Ministries provides a residential counseling setting for adolescents in crisis situations. With a capacity for 48 co-ed residents, Heartlight offers intense, individual attention that fosters an atmosphere of relationships. This interaction with staff, residents and other families provides an arena for change and a chance to gain wisdom, support, and encouragement through difficult times.

When situations of divorce, death, abuse, social difficulties, academic struggles, adoption issues and unhealthy coping mechanisms (lying, selfishness, manipulation, entitlement, depression, lack of motivation, disrespect for authority, confusion) are present, Heartlight offers an answer when removal from the home is necessary. Founded in 1989, the Heartlight program has proven successful in the lives of hundreds of teens and their families.

CREATES AN ARENA FOR change

Parenting Resources from Heartlight

When Your Teen Is Struggling

You've tried everything you know to do. Mark Gregston offers this encouragement: Don't lose hope. This groundbreaking book offers a system for helping kids work through their pain and offers hope and direction to parents looking for help. It will help you uncover and deal with the real issues causing your teen's troublesome behavior and offers tools for rebuilding healthy relationships.

"Mark Gregston offers parents relevant and effective help in a painful world for today's teens."
–Jon Rivers, KLOVE Radio

Published in 2007 by Harvest House. 215 pages softcover.

Belief System Workbook and CD

Workbook and audio training from Mark Gregston on how to successfully develop a Belief System for your home. The exercise will pull your family together under common banner of proper discipline and expectations. You'll learn how to create healthy rules and effective consequences and then properly communicate them to every member of the family.

"The Family Belief System is like a procedures and policies manual for your home. It is a critical component for parenting teenagers who want to push the limits."
– Mark Gregston

Library-style album includes a 38-page workbook, 70-minute instructional CD, worksheets, refrigerator magnets, table card, sticky reminder notes, and exclusive access to online materials, templates and examples.

Visit our online store at
www.heartlightresources.com
or call us toll-free at
866-700-FAMILY (3264).

HeartlightResources
FOR PARENTS

Parenting Resources from Heartlight

Dealing with Struggling Teens (seminar on video)
This 10-hour video recording on 5 DVDs is taught by Mark Gregston, who offers successful insights for handling teens who are spinning out of control. It is a convenient way for parents to learn from one of today's leading experts on teenage behavior when they feel like their teen is headed for disaster. Mark shares practical tips and steps to successfully deal with the conflicts a parent is having with a teen.

Dealing with Struggling Teens (seminar on audio)
The audio version of the popular live and video seminar by the same title is convenient for listening at home, work, or in the car. Buy for a loved one who is struggling with their teen. Includes 8 audio cds.

Visit our online store at
www.heartlightresources.com
or call us toll-free at
866-700-FAMILY (3264).

Parenting Resources from Heartlight

Parent Survival Kit
Our parent help library! Get the best of help rushed to you via expedited delivery. Includes all of our bestselling resources:

Dealing with Struggling Teens video seminar (5 DVDs)

Disciplining Your Teen audio set (6 CDs)

Parenting Through the Pain audio set (5 CDs)

Is Your Teen Spinning Out of Control? audio set (4 CDs)

When Your Teen is Struggling book

Belief System Workbook and CD

Plus, all 10 pocket books.

"Thank you so much!! The materials are just wonderful, and have brought tears to my eyes since I wished I had ordered them long ago."

–Teresa

The Parenting Teens Library
A library of 10 critical pocket books (50-150 pages each) written by Mark Gregston to answer the questions parents of teens are most asking today.
My Teen and the Internet
Implementing Change & Avoiding Chaos
Parenting Through the Pain
My Teen is Spinning Out of Control!
Secrets to Parenting Teens
Disciplining Your Teen
Preparing for the Difficult Years
The Phenomenon of Cutting
A Look at Adoption...from the Other Side
When Your Prodigal Won't Leave Home

Each of these pocket books can also be ordered individually.

Visit our online store at www.heartlightresources.com or call us toll-free at 866-700-FAMILY (3264).

HeartlightResources
FOR PARENTS

The live seminar for churches ...

Invite Mark Gregston to bring his popular seminar to your church. The live seminar is designed to help parents, leaders, and youth workers understand the world of today's teens and how to deal with them when they struggle.

...is now available on video for small groups!

The same seminar as Mark teaches live can now be enjoyed by your small group. It's a complete seminar in a box, including a workbook, leader's guide, promotional materials, posters, and eight 20-minute lessons on DVD.

Learn more at our website or call 866-700-FAMILY.

What Every Parent Needs to Know!

Presented By
Mark Gregston

dealing WITH **TODAY'S TEENS**
A SEMINAR FOR PARENTS AND YOUTH WORKERS

"For parents ready to admit they need guidance with managing their teen there is no one more qualified to learn from than Mark Gregston."

AN 8-LESSON VIDEO SEMINAR

www.dealingwithtodaysteens.org

Help is just a phone call away

Family Crisis Coaching from Heartlight offers a voice of hope, and is a place to turn when you're seeking direction for dealing with a struggling, rebellious or distant teen.

every day, hundreds of parents search for help for their teenager's problems. Many don't know what to do or where to turn when their family is turned upside down by a rebellious or self-destructive teen.

Family Crisis Coaching offers help to families caught in these situations. Our coaches are experts in dealing with teens who are out of control and they'll help you defuse the situation and bring sanity back to your home.

This service is a pre-counseling solution for parents. We'll make sure you get started on the right footing with a local counselor, if further help is needed.

Family Crisis Coaching also offers placement advice and assistance for those who may be considering placing their teen in a program outside of the home. Our coaches will guide you in making those decisions if the situation warrants it.

Most of all, you'll gain peace of mind and renewed hope, knowing our coaches have successfully dealt with situations just like yours, again and again. They'll be able to discern whether the behavior you're experiencing can be dealt with through new parenting tactics, or if it is dire enough to demand immediate professional attention.

FAMILY CRISIS COACHING

1-866-700-FAMILY (3264)
903-668-2173

HEARTLIGHT WEBSITES

Heartlight Residential Counseling
www.heartlightministries.org

Parenting Today's Teens Radio
www.parentingtodaysteens.org

Heartlight Resources
www.heartlightresources.com

Families in Crisis Coaching
www.familycrisiscoaching.com

Parenting Today's Teens Articles
www.markgregston.com

Families in Crisis Conference
www.familycrisisconference.com

Heartlight Radio
www.heartlightradio.org

Dealing With Today's Teens
www.dealingwithtodaysteens.org